MW01289674

CHECK YOUR REALITY

Transforming Distorted Thinking
For Lasting Empowerment & Well-Being

A Mental Health Primer

Brian M. Keltner

Contents

INTRODUCTION 7
- The Power of Our Thoughts 12
- "The Earth Is Flat" 17
- "I Am Powerless" 18
- Ancient Stoic Roots,
  Modern Mental Health 21
- Pulling the Wool Aside 22

PART 1: Distorted Thinking Patterns
- 1 - "Blaming the Victim" 29
- 2 - "Catastrophizing" 34
- 3 - "Denial" 39
- 4 - "Disqualifying the Positive" 43
- 5 - "Emotional Reasoning" 47
- 6 - "Entitlement" 52
- 7 - "Fallacy of Change" 56
- 8 - "Fallacy of Fairness" 61
- 9 - "I Can't" 67
- 10 - "Jumping to Conclusions" 71
- 11 - "Justification" 76

Contents

- 12 - "Magical Thinking"   81
- 13 - "Magnification & Minimization"   86
- 14 - "Overgeneralizing"   90
- 15 - "People-Pleasing"   94
- 16 - "Perfectionism"   99
- 17 - "Personalizing"   105
- 18 - "Polarizing"   110
- 19 - "Shoulds & Shouldn'ts"   114
- 20 - "Victim Stance"   119
- 21 - "Wishful Thinking"   123

PART 2: Distorted Thinking Transformation
- 1 - Self-Awareness   133
- 2 - Practicing Self-Awareness   137
- 3 - Applying Self-Awareness   143
- 4 – Distorted Thought Challenge   147
- 5 – Realizing the Change   153

CONCLUSION   159

Acknowledgments   167

About the Author   169

Preface

How's your quality of life these days?

While perfect satisfaction is illusory, we can still take a full measure of contentment. But a change in thinking may be needed.

As a psychotherapist, I enjoy a unique perspective on how much our sense of well-being depends on the makeup of our *thoughts*. Even education, job, income, assets, marital status, and geographic residence, though impactful, are surpassed. Unfortunately, many of us assume we're stuck with problematic perceptions for good. But that is false.

The methods discussed herein are ones I've used successfully with clients; I've also benefitted from them myself. It is evident that good mental health stems from psychological skills we all can learn. The old adage applies: "Give someone a fish and you feed them for a day; teach someone to fish and you feed them for a lifetime." This book teaches you to fish. It supplies rod, reel, and fly (or hook, line, and sinker if that's your thing). You provide intention, effort, and resolve in making the cast.

So I've prepared this course for ready digestion. First, the Introduction explores our thoughts' unique role in how we perceive and respond to reality; outlines the applicable psychological framework; and presents the markers and consequences of distorted thinking. Part I details 21 common distorted thinking patterns we all encounter in our lives. Part II explains how to transform this peculiar aspect of the human experience. Last, the Conclusion ponders a crucial question raised in studying this subject; it also throws down a challenge.

My hope is that you will come to regard this book as familiar. As you internalize its concepts, they will increasingly resonate. Above all, I hope you enjoy this exploration of the mind. It could be among the most important journeys of your life.

Brian M. Keltner, MA, LPC, NCC
Denver, Colorado

CHECK

YOUR

REALITY

GNOTHI SEAUTON

•

KNOW THYSELF

Ancient Greek
Aphorism Inscribed
On the Delphic
Temple of Apollo,
From an Ancient
Egyptian Proverb:
"Know thyself,
And ye shall know
The gods."

Everything we hear is an opinion, not a fact.
Everything we see is a perspective, not the truth.

Marcus Aurelius
(121 – 180 C.E.)

INTRODUCTION

Everything hangs on one's thinking.

Seneca (4 B.C.E. – 65 C.E.)

Man is disturbed not by things, but by the views he takes of them.

Epictetus (55 - 135 C.E.)

STORIED CENTURIES AGO, Italian Venice adopted a Moore as its favored son. While this was unprecedented, it was not unwarranted. He was an acclaimed Commander with many victories. Social standing was his despite humble origins. And a noblewoman whose love for him matched her fair beauty was his consort.

Above all, the popular persuasion held that the Moore was well endowed—with a noble mind. For everyone knew him to be true in intention, steadfast in duty, and romantic in affection. If he also was prideful, and bore insecurity about his race in a city notorious for its prejudice, still his position seemed unassailable.

But human nature is inevitable. And the Moore's adversaries weren't only on the battlefield. Some envied his ability, others resented his authority, and many frowned upon his marriage. Yet his worst foe was in his own ranks. Belying honest appearances, this trusted ensign was in truth a villain whose cunning hid his malevolence and whose ambition drowned his conscience.

Thus he insinuated in the Moore's mind that his spouse had been unfaithful. Although this was a lie, the insecure Moore believed it. Finally overcome by jealousy and rage, he strangled her to death with his own hands even as she pleaded her innocence. Only then, when it was too late, did he realize the truth before killing himself in a paroxysm of remorse.

°

Sound familiar? While Shakespeare's *Othello* is one of the more dramatic versions of this kind of tragedy, its variations have unraveled in life and art throughout human history. Essentially it is a cautionary tale about how illusion can wreck our lives if we aren't careful. And the illusion starts with what we *think*.

THE POWER OF OUR THOUGHTS

From the time humans first left footprints on the earth, we have sought to understand, to *know*. Asking "why?" was instinctive.

The natural world, for instance, held mysteries for our earliest ancestors that they needed to solve. Why did lightning and thunder fracture the sky, or rain and wind scour the land? Why did volcanoes shower the countryside with molten fire and ash? Why did the ground quake as though shaken by giant hands? Why did the stars form familiar shapes in the heavens—an archer, a scorpion, a winged horse, among so many others? Why did the sun track its ecliptic with seemingly divine precision? Why did moon pass before sun until midday became twilight? Why did comets rake the celestial dome like otherworldly harbingers?

Moreover, our innate social makeup has driven us to map the labyrinth of human intercourse. This includes overtures, intentions, and motivations *(How should I relate to her? Does he mean harm? Why did they do that?)*; worth and status *(Am I important? Do people care about or respect me? Will I be remembered?)*; and emotional experiences *(How am I feeling? Why do I feel this way? How would I feel if that happened to me? What are her feelings about this? How might he feel if that happened to him?)*. And beyond these intrigues have always loomed the ultimate mysteries: *Who am I? Why am I here? How long will I live? What happens to me after I die?*

In trying to answer such questions, ancient peoples reached their own conclusions about the nature and significance of things. These were gleaned from the evidence they saw around them as well as through their restless imaginations and emotional needs, hopes, and fears. Thus were created the myths and superstitions that offered a sense of understanding about the world in which they lived. Through such was perceived a cosmic order to which they were central, and over which they could exert control. Now they *knew*. And things finally made sense.

Today we recognize that this insatiable need to understand is a consequence of our intelligence. But it also helps us to meet life's challenges. Existence on this planet has always posed formidable problems; solving them has always required vast cognitive power. Thus our *thoughts* (beliefs, perspectives, opinions, and the significance we attribute to things) are the primary tool we use in this endeavor because they are the vehicle through which we reason, know, and act.

In addressing various concerns of our lives, the mind seems to operate in a typical way. First we try to determine the nature of a situation facing us. For example, if a stranger approaches we might ask ourselves, "Is this person a threat?" Next, we reach a perspective that seems right or makes sense. This is usually, though not always, influenced by evidence around us. We might notice, for instance, that the stranger is smiling in a friendly manner and decide, "This person isn't a threat." Last, we respond in a way reflecting our perspective. In this case relief or curiosity would be natural upon seeing that the stranger poses no danger. These emotions would likely compel us to return the stranger's smile and say, "Hi!"

Note the three elements of this process:

- <u>Thought</u>: *"This person isn't a threat."*
- <u>Emotion</u>: Curiosity; Relief
- <u>Behavior</u>: Smiling, saying "Hi!"

But that is only the beginning. Most significantly, our every response is encumbered by subjectivity. Take anger for example: we perceive a threat, feel that galvanizing emotion, and then act—even if a "threat" doesn't exist! Our perception presumes that it does and we respond accordingly. (If you've ever become angry about something that you later realized was harmless or imaginary, then you've experienced this firsthand.)

Consider the implications. Have you ever blamed your own emotional reactions on other people or situations? *"He/she/it/they made me feel this way!"* is the common refrain. This notion would have us believe that the origins of our emotions lie outside ourselves. If this were true, wouldn't everyone who shared an experience have the same emotional reaction just as gravity binds us all indiscriminately? Yet this doesn't happen. Instead people experience varied emotional responses to the same occurrence depending on their psychological perspectives of it. These emotions, in turn, motivate their behaviors.

Recalling the comet above, for instance, people have held wildly different interpretations of its advent throughout history to the present day: *It's the end of the world! The beginning of a new age! The coming of a god! A sign of good luck! A mass of ice and dust reflecting sunlight along its gravitational trajectory through space!* From such have come various emotional reactions: Fear, joy, wonder, elation, or curiosity. These in turn have provoked disparate behaviors: Mass suicide, mass celebration, mass propitiation, wagering frenzies, or field trips to the observatory.

Clearly, what we feel and do about everything encountered in life stems from our perceptions. This understanding compels two undeniable conclusions: *1) Our thoughts reflect our <u>perception</u> of what is real or true, which becomes our "reality"*; and *2) Our thoughts create our emotions, which in turn motivate our behaviors, in order to address this "reality."*

THOUGHTS create **EMOTIONS**
EMOTIONS motivate **BEHAVIOR**
To address
"REALITY"

What is "reality"? For our purposes it is neither the concreteness of the physical world nor the speculations of philosophy and religion, but rather the subjective product of our *thoughts* about what is real or true regarding ourselves, others, circumstances, and the world.

> **"REALITY"**: *The subjective product of our thoughts about what is real or true.*

This mental phenomenon is typified by skewed assessment because we don't always know someone's intentions or a situation's causes. Consequently we apply false *assumptions* and detrimental *bias*. This results in irrational or problematic thinking. Put another way:

Our **"REALITY"** isn't always the **REALITY**

Imagine these scenarios: 1) Someone cuts us off in traffic; 2) Our spouse fails to call at the agreed time; 3) Another applicant gets the job we wanted; 4) A group of people starts to laugh as we enter the room; 5) We hear strange noises in a dark house.

What do they have in common? As with many situations in our lives, their cause is open to interpretation because we don't necessarily know why they happened. Yet we experience an overwhelming need for answers. In fact we would rather feel certainty about things even at the risk of being wrong, than uncertainty in the recognition that *we don't know*. This is understandable given the reassurance such certainty offers; but it also creates problems.

Depending on what we decide is "really" going on, we will emotionally respond and then act in a way that feels appropriate or justified. Many times we'll assume the worst when we have no evidence for it. As a result, our emotions will be distressing while our behaviors may be destructive.

Take the first scenario: *Someone cuts us off in traffic.* Why does this happen? Perhaps the driver is swerving to avoid a hazard we can't see. We could be in their blind spot. Occasionally a general hostility ensnares us. There may be other reasons as well. Still, we tend to believe that we know exactly why it occurred and think, "*That asshole cut me off on purpose!*" It's no wonder we respond so often with frustration or rage. With that perception of "reality," why wouldn't we?

On the other hand, what if we knew that the driver in this case was a frantic mother rushing her dying son to the hospital, and that she didn't mean to cut us off? We would probably react differently.

So the reality is that we often get our "reality" wrong. And as a species we always have.

"THE EARTH IS FLAT"

This primitive notion may have begun with the sun as early humans watched it sink beyond the seemingly flat horizon at day's end, only to see it rise from the opposite horizon the next morning.

Considering that the earth looked flat from their vantage point, that the law of gravity hadn't yet been codified (which later explained why everything on the planet's surface stayed put as if on a shell), and that explorers who went beyond those far horizons often never returned, they drew a conclusion that seemed logical to them: the earth *was* flat, and if they traveled far enough they would fall off the edge.

As far as they were concerned this was a *fact*. Upon that soft foundation they built a slipshod edifice reflecting their "reality": Certainty about the shape of their world; anxiety around traveling too far; tales of adventurers who reached "the ends of the earth"; maps illustrating these supposed geographical limits; myths memorializing their flat earth's creation, and so on.

Yet that belief was incorrect; worse, it was limiting. With the result that human knowledge, which later grew exponentially from our discovery that the earth is round, was arrested for thousands of years. Imagine if you believed that the end of your neighborhood block marked the limits of where you could travel, explore, and settle. What impact would that have on your ability to understand the true nature of the world and your possibilities within it? How would such a belief affect your life choices?

Nevertheless to mock our ancestors from the high horse of hindsight is not the goal; they did their best with the knowledge they had, just as we do. The point is to reiterate that our thoughts shape notions of what is real or true in a given circumstance, thus dictating our emotions and behaviors as they arise to address that "reality."

This example also shows that our thoughts can give us false notions of what is real or true because of the inevitable limits on our perspective. We are not omniscient, after all.

"I AM POWERLESS"

Such a notion is all-too-common in the human experience. Often it starts at childhood—a stage when much of the psychological framework is built for our sense of what is real or true about ourselves, others, circumstances, and the world.

That this phase of life is rich soil for such thinking is no coincidence. Children view their environment as formidably complex, defying control, and governed by all-powerful adults. They are also innately dependent psycho-emotionally; and their egocentricity makes them assume they are the reason for so many of their experiences.

Imagine these conditions further compounded by overprotective parents. Their misguided if well-intentioned notions of love typically compel them to shelter their child from all possible hurt while providing for their every want or need. This is precisely to the child's detriment, ironically, as it undermines a wiser instinct to grab handfuls of unadulterated life experience toward acquiring knowledge, skills, experience, and self-confidence. Or involve violent or neglectful parents instead. While the former exert malicious control, the latter abandon the child to an environment that repeatedly frustrates attempts to negotiate it without guidance.

Trapped in those circumstances, the child tries to understand them by asking that fundamental question "Why?" Yet this understanding isn't reached through objective academic logic but rather subjective psycho-emotional "logic" applied through an egocentric mindset and derived from circumstantial "evidence," imagined "truths," and emotional imperatives. The conclusion reached by the child, though reflecting psychological naivete and perceptual error, offers an explanation for why things are the way they are: *"I am powerless."* Now the child *knows*, and things finally make sense.

This thinking will impact the child's mental health significantly. If he or she is fortunate enough to have psychological resiliency as well as some beneficial experiences, the powerlessness belief may be somewhat mitigated in adulthood. Still, ailments such as depression, anxiety, chronic anger, addiction, or codependency would be expected. These are all too real even as they stem from a perception that turns reality on its head. Because the truth is that total powerlessness is an illusion. Not even captivity negates the ability to choose an empowering perspective of one's circumstance, which determines how one feels about and copes with it. In contrast, the powerlessness belief enslaves one to a "reality" of one's own making.

Viewing things in such ways is called "Distorted Thinking." It is like looking (seeking to understand, to *know*) through a lens (thoughts, beliefs, perceptions, attitudes, and opinions) that is misshapen (irrational, assumptive, biased), and seeing a distorted image (reaching a dysfunctional, self-defeating, or otherwise compromised conclusion).

"DISTORTED THINKING": *Viewing things through an irrational, assumptive, or biased perspective to reach dysfunctional, self-defeating, or otherwise compromised conclusions.*

Simply being human seems to compel this tendency. If unaddressed, it will persist. And whether from curiosity, frustration, or resolve we've pondered it for thousands of years.

ANCIENT STOIC ROOTS, MODERN MENTAL HEALTH

In the 21st Century, our understanding that thoughts create emotions which in turn motivate actions seems like common sense. We can appreciate the elegant logic of this psychological order. And we recognize that those elements don't magically spring from gods or spirits or "the ether" but from our own minds.

Yet our species hasn't always known this. In fact, when ancient Greek philosophers first grasped this mental process over two millennia ago the insight was revolutionary. They eventually formed a way of life around it that lasted over a thousand years. Stoic—a reference to the *Stoa Poikile*, or Painted Porch, at Athens where it was first taught—was their name, and Stoicism their path.

Founded by Zeno of Citium in the third century B.C.E. and later espoused by such figures as Epictetus, Seneca, and Marcus Aurelius, Stoicism asserted that constructive emotions and behaviors were achieved through rational and unbiased thinking; therefore destructive emotions and behaviors stemmed from errors in judgment. It also recognized that human beings had the ability to observe, and thus determine the character of, their own thoughts. From practicing such observation, Stoics found, came the self-awareness needed to adjust their thinking. This led to tranquil feelings which compelled wise actions.

In the 1950s, psychologist Dr. Albert Ellis took inspiration from Classical Stoicism to create Rational Emotive Behavioral Therapy (REBT). This would later become a category of Cognitive Behavioral

Therapy (CBT) developed by psychologist Dr. Aaron Beck in the 1960s.*

These approaches assert that emotional and behavioral problems stem from the nature of people's thoughts about themselves, others, circumstances, and the world. Accordingly any irrational, assumptive, or biased thought creates a distorted view (of both the objective world around us and the subjective realm of *opinion* wherein an empowering perspective is more "rational" than a defeatist one because it nurtures psychological well-being). This results in compromised emotions and behaviors.

DISTORTED THINKING
Compromises
EMOTIONS and **BEHAVIORS**
To poorly address
REALITY

How can we manage this tendency? As ancient Stoicism held and modern psychology confirms, the first step is to identify it. And a more challenging task is difficult to find.

PULLING THE WOOL ASIDE

Despite its pernicious effects, distorted thinking camouflages itself from ordinary awareness. First, because such thinking is habitual it feels natural whether or not it is beneficial. Often we'll take it for granted or remain oblivious as if on autopilot. We may even resign ourselves to it because "that's just who

---

* CBT's "Cognitive Distortions," on which the Distorted Thinking Patterns in Part 1 are based, enjoyed widespread popularity after the publication of *Feeling Good: the New Mood Therapy* by David D. Burns, M.D. (Dover, 1980).

I am." For instance, are you self-critical whenever you make a mistake? Do you bother to question the validity of this criticism, or recognize its demoralizing effects on yourself? Are you just getting by with the feelings of guilt, shame, worthlessness, depression, or anxiety that commonly result from such thinking? Can you accept that there is more than one way to view a mistake, and that the very concept of "mistake" is arbitrary—a notion you don't necessarily have to live with?

Second, we affirm our own thinking—*our* version of "reality"—because it gratifies us to believe that it alone is right. After all (we ask ourselves), why would we purposely think something that is "wrong" or "dysfunctional"? In our minds that would be stupid and shameful to admit. Yet which is more foolish: Acknowledging our distorted thinking so we can transform it; or stubbornly denying our error so we can indulge that "special" view?

Third, we cling to perspectives held *at the time* as being sensible or correct, particularly amidst crises or trauma. Yet such thinking often remains stuck in the moment that compelled it while time passes and circumstances change. As children, for example, we might have responded to bullying by deciding that *"people are mean."* This belief could have led us to spend more time alone to avoid further harassment. Given the child's limited psycho-emotional resources and rudimentary social skills, such avoidance would have been understandable if not beneficial. Yet if such a belief were to last into adulthood, likely causing unhappiness and poor physical health from social isolation, that avoidant behavior would have become self-defeating because of the inevitable change in one's circumstances and the now-possible adult response.

Last, distorted thoughts formed by even dubious encounters with authority figures seem "normal" to us because their legitimacy is assumed. A child routinely abused at home, for instance, likely won't question their own beliefs of powerlessness, worthlessness, or other fettered notions that such treatment instills. This aspect of distorted thinking also occurs among mass populations in the form of harmful cultural norms. Patently outrageous customs such as cannibalism, human sacrifice, slavery, religious torture, genital mutilation, genocide, child marriage, and prejudice of all stripes have been perpetuated by various societies throughout human history up to the present day via questionable belief systems reinforced by authority structures. Yet such are still seen by their adherents as acceptable, beneficial, or even morally superior!

Thus the damage done by distorted thinking is undeniable. Via cascading effect it projects in our minds a false "reality." This impairs our ability to understand ourselves, others, circumstances, and the world in the most rational, objective, or empowering way. Consequently we feel distressing, crippling, or otherwise compromised emotions. These motivate abusive, self-defeating, or otherwise dysfunctional behaviors. The ensuing wreckage encompasses broken relationships, abandoned goals, lost hopes, forgotten dreams, pernicious customs, dubious traditions, and a degraded quality of life.

But we have an alternative. In recognizing our distorted thinking, we will likely want to change it because nothing is more important to us than being able to love our loved ones, respect ourselves and others, solve our problems, and feel happier in our lives.

Time to begin.

PART 1

DISTORTED THINKING PATTERNS

None are more hopelessly enslaved
Than those who falsely believe they are free.

Goethe (1749 – 1832 C.E.)

1

"BLAMING THE VICTIM"

Definition: *Assigning responsibility for harm to its casualty instead of its cause.*

Common Manifestations:
- Abusive family dynamic in which blaming the victim becomes normalized by the abuser to shift responsibility, condone abuse, and gain power and control. Children raised in such families often adopt this mindset in their own adult relationships.

- Instances of domestic violence, rape, and hate-crimes wherein the victim's gender, religion, profession, race, even clothing are implicated.

- Self-Recrimination after someone wrongs us.

- Presumption of religious, spiritual, or mystical "knowledge" through such notions as "karma" or "divine punishment" about people's suffering and misfortune (natural disasters, wartime atrocities, poverty, illness, etc.).

- Lack of empathy.

Sample Distorted Thoughts/Beliefs*:
- *"She asked for it by wearing that!"*
- *"They made themselves easy targets."*
- *"He needed to be taught a lesson."*
- *"It was her fault for being naïve."*
- *"They got in the way."*
- *"No one is a victim unless they allow it."*
- *"My spouse wouldn't hit me unless it was my fault."*
- *"It was their karma to be enslaved."*
- *"The tsunami was God's punishment of those people."*

*Note: Contextual intent is key. For instance, *"She needed to be taught a lesson"* would be a form of blaming the victim as epilogue to abusing one's wife. Conversely the same thought, reflecting a benign approach, would be quite reasonable in formal education.

Typical Resulting Emotions:
- Contempt
- Shame

- Self-Righteousness
- Smugness
- Disgust
- Vindictiveness
- Suspicion
- Arrogance
- Anger
- Dismissiveness

Example: *"She asked for it by wearing that!"* creates CONTEMPT which leads to condemning a woman for having been raped.

§

"The Nurse Accused"
An Illustration

*T*HE DAY FINALLY CAME when crime swallowed a deliberative justice system. "We need expediency!" the people cried.

After debate they decided the surest expediency meant punishing the victim. None could deny that arresting the victim would be expedient when the perpetrator couldn't be found. Certainly none could deny that charging the victim would be expedient when the perpetrator employed a stout legal defense.

Finally none could deny that condemning the victim would be expedient, without which no crime could have been committed.

So this new law was passed. Immediately arrests doubled as investigations became passé. Convictions tripled as jury deliberations were now a farce. It was quite the watershed moment.

Shortly thereafter, a young nurse working the downtown graveyard shift was savagely raped by an unknown subject. But instead of decrying this outrage, the people celebrated. "This crime would have overwhelmed the system before!" they crowed.

Now punishment came swiftly as the nurse was arrested and taken to court. "Is it not true," began the prosecutor, "that you chose to work a risky shift in a dangerous part of town?" The nurse replied that it was the only shift available, and the hospital couldn't be moved. "Is it not also true," continued the prosecutor, "that your clothing accentuated your shapely figure?" The nurse stated that the hospital required the uniform. "And is it not, finally, true," said the prosecutor, "that you invited the attack against you by being a woman?" The nurse pointed out that her gender had been decided before she was even born.

Not surprisingly the jury sent the young nurse to prison. And the people celebrated! Because, once upon a time, their deliberative justice system had been swallowed by crime but now it was expedient.

Point: Charging the hen with feeding itself to the fox is asinine on its face.

2

"CATASTROPHIZING"

Definition: *To perceive difficulty, failure, or disaster despite absent or contrary evidence.*

Common Manifestations:
- Fear of the unknown.

- Panic/confusion about life situations that one believes can't be handled or is "too good for."

- Unresolved past trauma.

- Belief that bad things are sure to happen in the future because they once happened in the past.

Sample Distorted Thoughts/Beliefs:

- *"Terrible things are going to happen!"*
- *"This is the worst thing that could have happened!"*
- *"There's no way I'll be able to handle this!"*
- *"I can't believe this is happening to <u>me</u>!"*
- *"I'll never get over it."*
- *"I had the worst childhood!"*
- *"I'm cursed!"*
- *"The sky is falling, the sky is falling!"*
- *"Getting out of bed in the morning is too much!"*
- *"If I don't eat/drink/buy this right now, I'll go crazy!"*

Typical Resulting Emotions:

- Fear/Panic
- Sadness
- Anxiety
- Resentment
- Depression
- Pessimism
- Anger
- Apathy
- Frustration
- Bitterness

Example: *"Terrible things are going to happen!"* creates ANXIETY which leads to never leaving the house.

"Tiffany and the Web"
An Illustration

A S WAS CUSTOMARY, Tiffany's parents worked long hours so she could have the best of everything.

This often left her home alone from a young age. She felt neglected at first, but her parents always said she was their first priority so acceptance followed. After all, didn't grownups pay attention to important things?

Before long, Tiffany's favorite pursuit was surfing the web. While her parents worked she spent hours at it, her impressionable mind absorbing the colorful media. Especially fun were snippets about twerking celebrities, and which models took the sexiest selfies or got butt implants, and how ugly was awful and beauty was fabulous.

She noticed other items too—about soldiers dying for hard-to-understand reasons in hard-to-pronounce places; or bankers gambling away their investors' money and getting a government "bail-out"; or the millions who lost everything in the economic crash; or the epidemic of gun deaths across the country; or the legalized corporate bribery of politicians; or the mass extinction caused by climate change.

The web had so many stories, in fact, that Tiffany felt confused about which were important. She wanted to ask her parents but they were too busy working. So she decided that the important ones were those she enjoyed the most—about twerking celebrities, and which models took the sexiest selfies or got butt implants, and how ugly was awful and beauty was fabulous.

By the time Tiffany was married with children, she considered herself fluent in things important. One day her six-year-old daughter ran to her crying "Mommy, the boys said my butt is flat!" Suddenly Tiffany panicked because she knew ugly was awful and beauty was fabulous. So she scheduled her daughter for a butt implant that week.

This made Tiffany feel better. After all, didn't grownups pay attention to important things?

Point: Where discernment is lacking, trivialities become crises while true crises are ignored.

3

"DENIAL"

Definition: *Failure to acknowledge harmful aspects of oneself, others, or circumstances.*

Common Manifestations:
- Aversion to losing a sense of security from something (relationship, status, drug, belief system) that is dysfunctional or self-defeating.

- Fear of change.

- Unawareness of one's distressing emotional states (such as unresolved anger, guilt, or grief).

Sample Distorted Thoughts/Beliefs:

- *"My husband hits me sometimes, but he's not abusive."*
- *"I drive better when I drink."*
- *"I don't need help!"*
- *"My body can handle two packs a day."*
- *"My daughter likes it when I touch her there."*
- *"Climate change is a myth."*
- *"Everything is fine!"*
- *"I don't get angry."*

Typical Resulting Emotions:

- Self-Righteousness
- Complacency
- Defensiveness
- Smugness
- Apathy
- Arrogance
- Grandiosity
- Stubbornness

Example: *"My husband only hits me now and then"* creates COMPLACENCY which leads to accepting an abusive marriage.

"Pharaoh and His Enemies"
An Illustration

IN EGYPT RULED A PHARAOH who loved to sit on the banks of the Nile like when he was a boy.

Each day, his eyes fixed on hippopotami splashing in fertile mud, barges drifting by, fishermen casting their nets, crocodiles rolling in the hunt, and the sun's molten reflection on the water.

One morning the pharaoh's advisor whispered urgently into his ear: the Nubian army was amassed on Egypt's border! But the pharaoh nodded absently as his mind lay with the Nile. So he made no overtures for peace; he devised no strategy for war; he raised no levies for his cities; he led no armies into battle. "There is no need," he mused, "the Nubians wouldn't dare cross our border."

A day passed before the pharaoh's advisor whispered again: the Nubians had crossed into Egypt! And again the pharaoh nodded and did nothing. "The Nubians wouldn't dare attack," he mused.

Hours later the pharaoh's advisor was back: the Nubians were attacking across Egypt! Yet again the pharaoh did nothing. "The Nubians," he mused, "wouldn't dare stay."

Before dawn the pharaoh's advisor whispered one last time: the Nubians were staying in Egypt—and coming for the pharaoh himself! While the pharaoh mused, "The Nubians wouldn't dare harm me."

But the Nubians dared, and struck down the pharaoh where he sat. Yet even in death his eyes fixed on hippopotami splashing in fertile mud, and barges drifting by, and fishermen casting their nets, and crocodiles rolling in the hunt, and the sun's molten reflection on the water.

Point: Dismissing a problem won't make it go away.

4

"DISQUALIFYING THE POSITIVE"

Definition: *Viewing good accomplishments, qualities, or circumstances as absent, trivial, or undeserved.*

Common Manifestations:

- Sabotage of oneself or others.

- Poor self-regard wherein the disqualification "confirms" such bias.

- Often accompanied by *always* and *never* (asserting unrealistic frequencies of occurrence and magnifying the sense of negativity out of all proportion).

Sample Distorted Thoughts/Beliefs:

- *"I never do anything right!"*
- *"Look at all the ones he got wrong!"*
- *"You always screw it up!"*
- *"It's our mistakes that count the most."*
- *"I always make mistakes!"*
- *"She never does it the right way!"*
- *"The world is a horrible place."*
- *"Life sucks!"*

Typical Resulting Emotions:

- Frustration
- Anger
- Hopelessness
- Anxiety
- Embarrassment
- Depression
- Disgust
- Shame
- Pessimism
- Arrogance
- Self-Recrimination
- Contempt
- Bitterness

Example: *"I never do anything right!"* creates HOPELESSNESS which leads to abandoning one's dreams or goals.

"Two Blind Women"
An Illustration

A BEAUTIFUL YOUNG WOMAN was born blind in one eye. Resenting this blemish, she perceived ugliness in her face and the world around.

Caught in the rain, she felt a chilling downpour. Walking among flowers, she smelled noxious weeds. Bathing in the sea, she feared murky depths. Crossing the desert, she saw a barren wasteland.

In time her resentment became rage. "How can I escape the ugliness?!" she cried, and plucked out her one good eye. But she soon realized in horror that her mind made her see as before.

This maddened her beyond reason. She became a vagabond, dirty and tattered. Her shapely face turned sunken, its empty eye socket gaping. People turned away as she approached, unwilling to look on her and unable to help. Finally destitute, she wandered for days until stumbling upon a seaside cottage.

"Is anyone home?" she cried.

"Yes, come in," replied the old woman who lived there. Her voice was kind, and conveyed a self-possession that comes from having learned hard lessons.

"I'm blind," said the young woman bitterly as she was seated by the hearth.

"So am I."

"Then you've escaped the ugliness?"

But the old woman smiled and shook her head. "Every day I enjoy the gentle rain, and the fragrant flowers, and the tranquil sea, and the vibrant desert," she said. "It's not so bad."

Then she touched the young woman's face with gentle, seeing hands. "How beautiful you are!" she marveled. And the young woman began to weep, for only then did she understand.

Point: To know the beauty around us, we must be willing to see it.

5

"EMOTIONAL REASONING"

Definition: *Basing choices solely on feelings despite the resulting abuse, self-sabotage, or destruction.*

Common Manifestations:

- Impulsivity

- Sense of power, control, or relief derived from emotional "venting" or "acting out."

- Undeveloped cognitive skills such as planning, problem-solving, response inhibition, delayed gratification, multi-perspective taking, and self-monitoring.

Sample Distorted Thoughts/Beliefs:

- *"It feels good to follow my feelings!"*
- *"My emotions are always right!"*
- *"I'm just being spontaneous!"*
- *"I have to break something to get rid of my anger!"*
- *"If the urge is strong then it must be right."*
- *"I must express my feelings this way."*
- *"Emotions always tell the truth."*

Typical Resulting Emotions:

- Recklessness
- Arrogance
- Grandiosity
- Stubbornness
- Euphoria
- Self-Righteousness

Example: *"I have to break something to get rid of my anger!"* creates RECKLESSNESS which leads to shattering another cell phone against the wall.

°

Note: The distinction between "Emotional Reasoning" and intuition (a.k.a. "gut feeling" or "hunch") is worth noting. Sometimes we make sound, quick decisions based on the latter; meanwhile the cognitions driving it are beyond our awareness such that the decision-making process seems emotional. This is natural and, at times, crucial.

Yet how often is what we commonly mistake for "intuition" simply wrong? Have you ever had a "gut feeling" about lottery numbers, a "hunch" about what someone did, or some other emotional certainty about how something happened, which turned out to be way off?

The quandary is that our intuition can be dead-on. Is it possible to develop into a reliable skill? Many would say so, and learn to trust it in certain situations for good reason. Still, our feelings are neither an infallible guide nor a kind of mystical "knowing" leading us unerringly to constructive ends. To the contrary, we can rely on emotional reasoning to push us toward undesirable destinations like a faulty compass.

§

"Impulse and the Traveler"
An Illustration

IN A TANGLED GREEN VALLEY sat the town of Impulse. "Do What You Feel Like" was its motto, for the inhabitants were like children.

Buildings were half-erected there. Road signs lay unfinished. Streets intersected with no sense of direction. Fences without buttressing swayed in the wind. Broken windows were a fixture, while the panes meant to replace them sat nearby unfitted. Outlying roads led haphazardly to a dead end or the cliff's edge.

Meanwhile the people of Impulse readily fulfilled their town's directive. They ran amok, throwing stones or starting fires or attacking each other at whim. One enterprising crew had begun to build a general store, though it would eventually join other structures half-built. Workers trudged from street to street with buckets of asphalt, partially filling potholes before bolting to drink and brawl. Inside broken homes, the petty bickering of husbands and wives drifted through town. While in back alleys the screams of violated women and degraded men pierced the broad day and narrow night.

And while these episodes were common, common too was regret about some unfinished task or destructive act, wasted time and wasted money. But then the people would recall their town motto, and things would make sense again and they'd feel better.

One day a traveler arrived from the far province of Reason. He was an old man wrapped in a cloak and gripping a staff; yet his stride was long, and his dark eyes captured his surroundings. Surveying Impulse's half-baked structures, unfinished signs, nonsensical streets, broken windows, and dead end roads he shook his head. Hearing the petty bickering of husbands and wives, he cringed. Assaulted by the screams of violated women and degraded men, he felt afraid.

Nevertheless he continued into town with a clear intent. Suddenly a half-naked man with blood on his lips attacked him with a club, beating him until he fell to the ground twisted and broken.

"Why did you do that?" the traveler gasped.

"Because I felt like it," said the man regretfully. But then he recalled his town motto, and things made sense again and he felt better.

Point: Feelings untended by reason are prone to stampede.

6

"ENTITLEMENT"

Definition: *Regarding oneself as better than others and deserving of special privilege at others' expense.*

Common Manifestations:
- Unhealthy psychological boundaries often learned from parents who rarely say "no" to their children or model lack of consideration.

- Self-indulgence seen as "reward" or "payback" for perceived wrongs or misfortunes.

- Irresponsible and potentially harmful actions such as drinking/texting and driving.

- Lack of empathy.

Sample Distorted Thoughts/Beliefs:

- *"I deserve more than others do."*
- *"I'm better than he/she is."*
- *"They don't matter as much as I do."*
- *"My wants and needs are special."*
- *"All that matters is I get what I want."*
- *"I deserve this for what I've been through."*
- *"Others need to follow the rules, not me."*
- *"People aren't as special as I am."*

Typical Resulting Emotions:

- Arrogance
- Self-Righteousness
- Smugness
- Recklessness
- Dismissiveness
- Contempt
- Grandiosity

Example: *"I deserve more than others do"* creates ARROGANCE which leads to embezzling from the company pension fund.

§

"The Child and His Wants"
An Illustration

*A*S AN INFANT, CHARLES got what he wanted every time he wanted it.

When hungry he would cry and be fed. When soiled he would cry and be changed. When frustrated he would cry and be picked up. When restless he would squirm and be put down. And he thought, "Now this is the life!"

By age two Charles was accustomed to getting what he wanted whenever he wanted it. So he would scream until getting to play, sulk until getting his toy, whine until mommy picked him up, struggle until daddy put him down. And he thought, "Now this is the life!"

In his teen years Charles realized that he could get what he wanted every time he wanted it. After wrecking his car he demanded another. After failing his classes he insisted on straight A's. After getting sick he craved others' pity. After getting well he pushed others away. And he thought, "Now this is the life!"

With the arrival of adulthood, Charles knew he deserved whatever he wanted whenever he wanted it. So he cheated on his wife when bored with her, yelled at his children when irritated with them, pouted to get attention, shouted to be left alone. And he thought, "Now this is the life!"

Point: Our self-absorbed predilections reflect a spoiled brat.

7

"FALLACY OF CHANGE"

Definition: *1) Belief that conforming to others' expectations leads to one's own satisfaction; OR 2) Assumption that others will conform to one's own expectations eventually.*

Common Manifestations:

- Relationship dynamic in which one turns the other into an "improvement project."

- Parental pressure on the child to become someone or something they, by nature or inclination, are not.

- Rejection of uniqueness or autonomy.

- A way of feeling more secure in a relationship by exerting power/control.

- Presumption that "success" (however defined) is achievable only one way.

- Lack of empathy.

Sample Distorted Thoughts/Beliefs:
- *"He'll be happier changing."*
- *"I know what's best for her."*
- *"My way is the best way."*
- *"People can't make good choices for themselves."*
- *"She's not okay as she is."*
- *"I'll be happier if I make him happy."*
- *"They'll see that changing is for the best."*

Typical Resulting Emotions:
- Self-Righteousness
- Arrogance
- Smugness
- Suspicion
- Stubbornness
- Dismissiveness
- Self-Doubt

Example: *"People can't make good choices for themselves"* creates ANXIETY which leads to micromanaging a relationship to death.

"Daddy's Little Girl"
An Illustration

DEEP IN THE FOREST lived a young girl in a cottage. Her mother had died giving birth to her, and she was left in her father's care.

In the girl's eyes her father towered over others like the trees. His hair was the color of wheat, and his face was tanned and sleek. Each morning, he awakened her with the earthy scent of daisies on her pillow. After frying pancakes on the griddle, he listened to her read before going to tend the peach orchard. Then he'd say, "Be good, my girl!" And his eyes shone like the sky while his stride resounded.

So clearly did he cherish her that she felt as loved when he left as when he returned. And she thought, "Someday I will marry a man like my father, and he'll make me happy."

Years passed, and the girl grew into a young woman. She was out walking through the orchard one day when she saw a figure who towered over others like the trees. His hair was the color of wheat, and his face was tanned and sleek. When he smiled, his eyes shone like the sky; and his stride resounded.

"Father!" she shouted, and ran forward. But then she realized he was only the neighbor boy grown into a young man. "Oh, it's just you," she said. Yet she felt nervous in his presence, and her breast heaved in anticipation. At that moment she knew he was the one she would marry.

And marry they did, soon after beneath the peach trees. The wedding guests marveled at how like her father the young man was, and how happy he would surely make her.

But as time went on, the young woman felt dissatisfied. Instead of daisies on her pillow her new husband awakened her with a kiss. Instead of pancakes on the griddle he fried steak and eggs. Instead of listening to her read he perused the morning paper. Instead of saying "Be good, my girl!" before going to the orchard, he kissed her softly and murmured, "I love you."

So clearly did he do things differently from her father that she felt as unloved when he returned as when he left. And she thought, "If only he did things like my father, he'd make me happy."

Consequently she started to complain. Whenever her husband kissed her in the morning, she complained until he put daisies on her pillow. Whenever he fried steak and eggs, she complained until he cooked pancakes on the griddle. Whenever he perused the morning paper, she complained until he listened to her read. Whenever he murmured "I love you" before going to the orchard, she complained until he said, "Be good, my girl!" But his eyes no longer shone like the sky, and his stride no longer resounded.

So clearly had he lost that manner reminiscent of her father that the young woman felt more unloved than ever—and she wept.

Point: Trying to change others "for the better" only makes things worse.

8

"FALLACY OF FAIRNESS"

Definition: *1) Equality expectation that is impossible; OR 2) Equality canard that serves only self.*

Common Manifestations:
- Self-interest masquerading as altruism.

- Vain idealism.

- Making one's happiness/satisfaction contingent upon perfect fairness.

- Lack of empathy.

Sample Distorted Thoughts/Beliefs:

- *"It's not fair that I had an unhappy childhood!"*
- *"Everyone gets what they deserve."*
- *"Why am I the only one who suffers?!"*
- *"If only life were fair, then I could be happy."*
- *"Life is fair (as long as I get what I want)."*
- *"Life's not fair!"*
- *"It's not fair that some people get all the breaks!"*

Typical Resulting Emotions:

- Bitterness
- Resentment
- Frustration
- Sadness
- Anger
- Arrogance
- Anxiety
- Pessimism
- Depression
- Hopelessness
- Self-Righteousness

Example: *"It's not fair that I had an unhappy childhood!"* creates BITTERNESS which leads to chronic griping.

○

Note: As we typically define "fair" (perfect equality for and among all based on some notion of "right"), life isn't and never has been. The strong and weak, large and small, fast and slow, tall and short, attractive and

62

plain, exceptional and mediocre, privileged and unfortunate have always been. Comparatively, one always has it "better" in some ways and "worse" in others. This reflects the diversity characteristic of life on this planet.

To complain about life's unfairness makes as much sense as resenting gravity's pull. Instead we have another choice: accept the reality of the moment, remind ourselves of what we *do* have, and use our time and energy toward improving our situation to the greatest possible extent.

§

"Two Sons and a Castaway"
An Illustration

ONE SPRING, A SON was born to a wealthy banker and his wife. Naturally they lavished upon him the best care they could afford.

As an infant, he was swaddled in silk and bathed in perfumed water. As a toddler, he was fed with a golden spoon engraved by artisans. As a child, he enjoyed Persian rugs to play on and private gardens to explore.

Now a schoolboy, he was driven each day to a private academy in a luxury sedan, wearing lambskin loafers and a cashmere suit. His neighbors envied him. They envied his spacious home because theirs were less spacious, his stylish clothes because theirs were less stylish, his luxury car because theirs were less luxurious. And they would whine, "That's not fair!" because they wanted what he had.

Yet despite his privilege, the banker's son felt unhappy. At school he was required to sit where his teachers told him to sit, speak when his teachers told him to speak, and be quiet when his teachers told him to be quiet, just like the other students. And he would whine, "That's not fair!" because at home he was used to special treatment.

Meanwhile, on the other side of town was born a son to a poor farmer and his wife. Naturally they too lavished upon him the best care they could afford. As an infant, he was swaddled in canvas and bathed in cloudy well-water. As a toddler, he was fed with a flat stick shaped by rough stones. As a child, he enjoyed a packed dirt floor to play on and fields of farmland to explore.

Now a schoolboy, he walked barefoot five miles each day to a public institution, wearing burlap trousers sewn with fishing line. His neighbors too envied him. They envied his small hut because theirs were smaller, his plain clothes because theirs were plainer, his road to school because theirs were longer. And they would whine, "That's not fair!" because they wanted what he had.

Yet despite his privilege, the farmer's son too felt unhappy. At school he was required to sit where his teachers told him to sit, speak when his teachers told him to speak, and be quiet when his teachers told him to be quiet, just like the other students. And he would whine, "That's not fair!" because at home he was used to special treatment.

One day after school the two boys were returning home, by luxury sedan and bare foot respectively. They happened to pass along the same stretch of road at the same moment and saw an old man sitting in the dirt. His beard was matted and his clothing soiled. Gnarled toes protruded from worn socks. He stank of sour wine and urine. And each boy thought to himself how unfair it was that he had to see such a sight as he went by.

Point: Our notion of "fair" is often narrow self-interest raising its ugly head.

9

"I CAN'T"

Definition: *Belief that some worthy, achievable pursuit is wrong or impossible.*

Common Manifestations:

- Lack of self-confidence wherein a task is seen as impossible to avoid feelings of inferiority, embarrassment, or shame about a lack of achievement.

- Ignorant, self-serving, or limiting notions of "right" imposed by authority figures.

- Clinging to established norms when a new way would lead to better outcomes.

Sample Distorted Thoughts/Beliefs:

- *"There's no way I can do this!"*
- *"Failure is inevitable."*
- *"It's wrong to go against your upbringing."*
- *"It can't be done!"*
- *"Nobody in their right mind would try that."*
- *"Some things are best left alone."*
- *"I'm better off not even trying."*
- *"Who am I to change the way things have always been done?"*
- *"Better safe than sorry."*

Typical Resulting Emotions:

- Fear/Panic
- Shame
- Guilt
- Frustration
- Pessimism
- Sadness
- Stubbornness
- Depression
- Timidity
- Anxiety
- Apathy
- Bitterness
- Self-Doubt

Example: *"Some things are best left alone"* creates TIMIDITY which leads to not asking for a well-deserved raise.

"Adventure and the Lady"
An Illustration

WHEN CLAIRE WAS LITTLE she loved splashing in mud puddles, climbing trees, and skipping along woodland trails. But each time she did her parents chided, "You can't Claire, it's not ladylike!"

At first Claire questioned this notion though doubt had been sown. So she still splashed and climbed and skipped but with waning enthusiasm. And her parents' chiding continued.

Eventually she gave in. Nearing a mud puddle, she stepped around it. Spying a tree, she turned away. Crossing a woodland trail, she plodded through it. And her parents were quite pleased.

Yet as Claire grew up, she imagined smashing old barriers despite herself. All-female SEAL teams, a woman as Pope, and the Women's Football League were long overdue! But then she remembered her parents' chiding. So while others reached for those breakthroughs, she did not. And her parents were quite pleased.

By the time adulthood settled in, Claire wasn't sure about what she could do; but she was certain about what she couldn't. "I can't," she'd say when invited to go swimming. "I can't," she'd say when invited to go climbing. "I can't," she'd say when invited to go hiking. And her parents were quite pleased.

Years later, Claire's children splashed in mud puddles, climbed trees, and skipped along woodland trails just as she once had. But having become a lady, she could only watch. And her parents were quite pleased.

Point: Beware your mind's echo of others' prohibitions!

10

"JUMPING TO CONCLUSIONS"

Definition: *Prejudging others' intentions, present circumstances, or future scenarios.*

Common Manifestations:
- "Fortune-telling": belief that one *knows* the future (often an attempt to feel more secure about coming events that are otherwise unpredictable or uncontrollable).

- "Mind-reading": belief that one *knows* the thoughts of others (often an attempt to cope with anxiety stemming from interpersonal uncertainty or mistrust).

- "Evidence" prompting dubious behaviors (such as cheating on a spouse first, whom one believes is inevitably going to cheat).

Sample Distorted Thoughts/Beliefs:
- *"I already know what's going to happen."*
- *"He/she is judging me!"*
- *"I know exactly what they're going to do."*
- *"It's just a matter of time before he/she hurts me."*
- *"I'm going to fail anyway, so why even try?"*
- *"The world is going to end anyway, so fuck it!"*
- *"I'll never be able to convince them."*
- *"He/she/they <u>meant</u> to hurt me!"*
- *"People are out to get me."*
- *"Nothing good will ever happen to me."*
- *"Those people are laughing at me."*

Typical Resulting Emotions:
- Fear/Panic
- Pessimism
- Anxiety
- Suspicion
- Depression
- Anger
- Jealousy
- Vindictiveness
- Stubbornness
- Self-Righteousness
- Bitterness
- Arrogance
- Paranoia

-Example: *"She's judging me!"* creates ANGER which leads to lashing out at one's lover for no good reason.

§

"The Gypsy and the King"
An Illustration

NOT LONG AGO lived a gypsy who believed she could read people's minds and tell their fortunes. Seeing an opportunity, she pitched a pavilion along the king's road with a sign advertising her talents.

Each day, hundreds of travelers noticed this new attraction. Some shook their heads and continued on; but others stopped in because they knew that one's mind could be tricky and fortunes were hard to come by.

In time the gypsy's fame grew. Yet folks couldn't agree on the genuineness of her talent. Some praised her as a magician while others condemned her as a charlatan. Still, her reputation preceded her throughout the kingdom.

One afternoon a bent and barefoot old man wearing a beard and rags shuffled into the gypsy's tent. Inside he saw a crystal ball atop a round wood table. Sitting next to it was the gypsy. Her flashing dark eyes and bejeweled fingers lent to her an air of mystery. But before the gypsy could prognosticate the old man said, "Give me your thoughts, madam, before you reveal mine; and tell me your own fortune before I give you a farthing."

Amused by the beggar's pluck, the gypsy played along. "Your poverty shall recede," she canted, "while my future's bright indeed!"

The old man offered a grim smile. "I don't think so," he said. Then he straightened to his full height and tore off his beard, which was pasted on. The gypsy gasped, for only then did she recognize the king. With a clap of his hands the king ordered his guards to arrest the gypsy as a fraud. Whereupon they bundled her in chains despite her protests, and led her struggling away.

Yet the king, lingering by the pavilion, felt pity. For he knew that one's mind could be tricky and fortunes were hard to come by.

Point: Think twice when certain you know what others are thinking.

11

"JUSTIFICATION"

Definition: *Condoning a behavior, circumstance, or consequence through pernicious, dysfunctional, or self-serving rationales.*

Common Manifestations:
- A means of avoiding anxiety, guilt, or shame that would otherwise result from questioning one's own dubious perspectives or choices.

- Invoking tradition, precedent, or authority to support a dubious status quo.

- Lack of empathy.

Sample Distorted Thoughts/Beliefs:

- *"The ends justify the means."*
- *"To make an omelet, you have to break a few eggs."*
- *"An eye for an eye."*
- *"I have to bet the house so my kids can go to college!"*
- *"I only <u>look</u> at child porn—I don't actually abuse those kids."*
- *"I know I was rough on her, but she pissed me off."*
- *"He/she started it!"*
- *"This is just how we do things."*

Typical Resulting Emotions:

- Arrogance
- Smugness
- Defensiveness
- Self-Righteousness
- Recklessness
- Stubbornness
- Vindictiveness
- Grandiosity

Example: *"I only look at child porn—I don't actually abuse those kids"* creates SELF-RIGHTEOUSNESS which leads to collecting media of children being raped.

§

"The Mayor and Her Citizens"
An Illustration

IN A SMALL COASTAL BURG resided a mayor who considered herself very important. After all, hadn't the people chosen her to govern them?

One day sheeting rain flooded the town. It left sinkholes and gaps where smooth streets had been. The mayor thought, "If I don't ensure my transportational welfare, the people will suffer." So she took funds from the town's coffers for an executive helicopter. "This," the mayor announced, "will ensure the people's safety against floods!" The people grumbled among themselves as they commuted on broken roads. But what could they do?

Soon a hurricane carved the town in a destructive swath. It left naked bricks and splintered wood where homes and businesses had stood. The mayor thought, "If I don't ensure my residential welfare, the people will suffer." So she took funds from the town's dwindling coffers for a grand estate. "This," the mayor announced, "will ensure the people's safety against hurricanes!" The people grumbled among themselves as they filed into homeless shelters. But what could they do?

Sometime later an earthquake shook the town like a shivering giant. Scarred roads tore apart, and homeless shelters collapsed along with other buildings. The mayor thought, "If I don't ensure my official welfare, the people will suffer." So she emptied the town's coffers to build a marble headquarters. "This," the mayor announced, "will ensure the people's safety against earthquakes!" The people grumbled among themselves as they moved into emergency tents. But what could they do?

Not long after, a severe hailstorm blew through. It shredded the people's flimsy suburbs, leaving them exposed and huddled together. The mayor thought, "If I don't ensure my citizens' welfare, the people will suffer." So she raised taxes to fill empty coffers. "This," the mayor announced, "will ensure the people's safety against hailstorms!"

The people grumbled among themselves as they knew the mayor's mind by now. Then they seized her in rage and tore her to pieces.

Point: Once too often we excuse inexcusable actions.

12

"MAGICAL THINKING"

Definition: *Attribution of mystical, supernatural, or otherworldly significance to a person, behavior, object, or characteristic.*

Common Manifestations:
- Pernicious superstition stemming from one's need to feel superior, powerful, or in control.

- Bizarre behaviors or rituals that are logically and causally disconnected from the benefits they supposedly bring.

Sample Distorted Thoughts/Beliefs:
- *"If I cut myself, I'll let all the pain/badness out of me."*

81

- *"I'll win the lottery if I use my special numbers."*
- *"Crystals will heal my sick baby."*
- *"Unbelievers are evil."*
- *"I'm cursed!"*
- *"Visualizing wealth will make me rich!"*
- *"Self-mutilation will purge my sins."*
- *"If I wear my lucky jersey, my team will win."*
- *"Whipping my children casts out the devil."*
- *"I'm just unlucky."*

Typical Resulting Emotions:
- Fanaticism
- Arrogance
- Stubbornness
- Hopelessness
- Anxiety
- Euphoria
- Complacency
- Grandiosity

Example: *"Visualizing wealth will make me rich!"* creates GRANDIOSITY which leads to being a potted plant instead of employed.

°

Note: An exploration of Magical Thinking naturally includes *superstition*. No doubt we've all engaged in such at some point: Wearing certain colors or clothing to "help" our sports team win; not walking under a ladder; knocking on wood; crossing our fingers while making a promise; sharing some obligatory meme on social media, and so on. Mostly we practice these rituals automatically, taking for granted their efficacy. Or we indulge them with a wink.

Yet the gradient leading from benign superstitions to malignant ones is steep. Backwardness tends to gain momentum once we start down it. Remember when bathing was considered unhealthy? Or "witches" were burned at the stake? Or science and medicine were condemned as evil? Or education was seen as a tool of the "Devil"? Whether from an urge to control, or a need to *know,* or simple ignorance, superstition has impeded our ability to address reality long before our ancestors bowed down to stone.

§

"The Mage and the Dice"
An Illustration

EACH YEAR, A MAGE made pilgrimage to that desert mecca where fortunes are won or lost by chance. And he always wore his magic ring, for did it not roll the dice his way?

Of course, he would admit reluctantly, sometimes the House cast spells on him with its complimentary drinks, meandering floors, and tacky décor. Then those numbered cubes rattled like dead bones as his luck vanished. Just the year before, events had gone so badly that he'd had to raid his retirement account to roll the dice again.

This night, guided by the glow of neon lights and gleaming towers, the mage arrived with the setting sun to stand before the table. His ring seemed to hum as the dice leaped from his hand—a winning throw! The mage smiled, twisting the ring around his finger as if opening a bottle of luck. He rolled again, this time a loss. Frowning, he knew the House was weaving its magic against him, and gulped his drink. Then he rolled again—a bigger loss this time!

Rubbing his ring as though it were Aladdin's lamp, the mage heard it whisper that all would be well—or did _he_ whisper it?— and flung the dice once more. His groan seemed disembodied to his ears as the croupier slid his final bet away. How had the money gone so quickly?!

Trudging once more from that desert mecca where fortunes are won or lost by chance, the mage vowed to return. And he would wear his magic ring again—for did it not roll the dice his way?

Point: In a world often beyond control, illusions of control are often self-defeating.

13

"MAGNIFICATION & MINIMIZATION"

Definition: *Misconstruing one's impact on others, others' impact on oneself, or a situation's true effects.*

Common Manifestations:

- Abusive relationships in which both parties minimize the abuse—the abuser to preserve power or view the abuse as acceptable, the abused to preserve the relationship out of unhealthy dependency or poor self-worth.

- "Revenge" scenarios wherein one magnifies a perceived offense in order to indulge a desire for disproportionate payback ("an eye for a tooth").

- Psychologically toxic family/work dynamics that one dismisses to avoid what would actually be beneficial conflict/change.

- Lack of empathy.

Sample Distorted Thoughts/Beliefs:
- *"I know my husband doesn't mean to hit me when he's angry."*
- *"People who think I'm an asshole need to get over it."*
- *"I should beat his ass for looking at me like that!"*
- *"In the grand scheme of things, it's not a big deal that my wife forgot our anniversary again."*
- *"My boss is just teasing when he smacks my butt."*
- *"How dare she disagree with me!"*
- *"I'm gonna key that asshole's car for parking too close!"*

Typical Resulting Emotions:
- Dismissiveness
- Complacency
- Anxiety
- Vindictiveness
- Recklessness
- Anger
- Arrogance
- Resentment
- Paranoia

Example: *"How dare she disagree with me!"* creates ANGER which leads to hitting one's daughter for having an opinion.

§

"Rex and His Hazards"
An Illustration

REX WAS DRIVING HOME in his beat-up blue pickup when he noticed a brown sedan following him.

"That asshole's about to rear-end me!" he thought, although the sedan wasn't that close. So he ground his foot into the brake pedal, causing the sedan to swerve into another car to avoid hitting him. "They'll get over it," Rex muttered as he continued home.

Several miles later a sporty white coupe raced by. "That asshole almost ran me off the road!" Rex thought, although the coupe hadn't come that close. So he ground his foot into the gas pedal to catch up, and jerked his steering wheel in the coupe's direction. This caused it to swerve into another car to avoid being hit.

"They'll get over it," Rex muttered as he continued home.

Only blocks from Rex's house, the red hatchback in front of him stalled as the light turned green. "That asshole's keeping me from getting home!" he thought, although the left lane was clear. So he ground his palm into the horn and strode to the hatchback wielding a crow bar. The car's elderly driver cringed at this onslaught, and began clutching his chest from a sudden heart attack.

"He'll get over it," Rex muttered as he climbed back into his truck and continued home.

Point: Raising mountains from molehills creates nasty weather.

14

"OVERGENERALIZING"

Definition: *Applying negative aspects of one person to whole groups or a single instance to many situations.*

Common Manifestations:
- Prejudice and stereotyping (race, religion, culture, politics, gender, class, etc.) in order to feel important or superior. This often masks feelings of inferiority or insignificance.

- Attempt to feel more emotionally secure through supposed "knowledge" of people or situations.

- Lack of empathy.

Sample Distorted Thoughts/Beliefs:

- *"All blacks are thugs."*
- *"All whites are racist."*
- *"All Jews are greedy."*
- *"All Muslims are terrorists."*
- *"All Mexicans are lazy."*
- *"Women are bitches."*
- *"Men are pigs."*
- *"Gays are child molesters."*
- *"You can't trust anybody."*
- *"People are all the same."*

Typical Resulting Emotions:

- Arrogance
- Self-Righteousness
- Contempt
- Vindictiveness
- Stubbornness
- Anxiety
- Hate
- Bitterness
- Anger
- Fear

Example: *"You can't trust anybody"* creates ANXIETY which leads to never making close friends.

§

"Workers and Laborers"
An Illustration

I N THE LAND OF OPPORTUNITY, Workers and Laborers comprised the two political parties. Although they were largely synonymous, each sold itself to voters as the land's best hope.

"Workers are Opportunity's salvation!" cried the Workers.

"Laborers are Opportunity's foundation!" cried the Laborers.

So the two parties were rivals. Both took credit when prosperity came, but blamed each other when conditions soured. Then legislators harangued from the lecterns while constituents quarreled in the taverns.

"Laborers are parasites!" cried the Workers.

"Workers are tyrants!" cried the Laborers.

Eventually the two parties became enemies. Enraged partisans armed themselves and faced off in the streets. Then they commenced slaughtering each other until Opportunity lay in bloody puddles.

"Death to the workers!" screamed the laborers.

"Death to the Laborers!" screamed the workers.

Finally the two parties were in tatters. Still, they breathed political life because nothing was left to replace them. And to no one's surprise, each sold itself to voters as the land's best hope.

Point: Name-calling incites prejudice over tolerance, and war instead of peace.

15

"PEOPLE - PLEASING"

Definition: *Prioritizing others while neglecting oneself to get love or approval.*

Common Manifestations:
- High-risk behaviors stemming from peer pressure (substance abuse, promiscuity, law-breaking, etc.).

- Consequence of parental withholding of love as punishment for the child's failure to gratify the parent's needs/wants. The child grows up believing that his or her own needs/wants are unimportant, and that others come first.

- Typically mistaken for being "nice," "polite," "generous," or "good."

- Emotional suppression (especially anger) when others fail to reciprocate.

Sample Distorted Thoughts/Beliefs:
- *"He won't like me unless I sleep with him."*
- *"She won't like me unless I buy her things."*
- *"I'm a bad person if I don't give people what they want."*
- *"I don't need anything."*
- *"Putting yourself first is selfish."*
- *"I'm okay with not getting anything in return."*
- *"It's better to give than receive."*
- *"You have to go along to get along."*
- *"Making other people happy is what matters."*

Typical Resulting Emotions:
- Anxiety
- Anger
- Fear/Panic
- Shame
- Guilt
- Timidity
- Depression
- Desperation
- Confusion
- Sadness
- Pride
- Self-Righteousness
- Self-Doubt

Example: *"She won't like me unless I buy her things"* creates DESPERATION which leads to spending money on expensive dinners, clothes, and jewelry until one is broke.

§

"The Model Child"
An Illustration

WHEN DOLORES WAS A GIRL, her parents quarreled until divorce ended their misery. Eventually her father stopped visiting, while her mother turned cold and distant.

Not surprisingly, Dolores felt confused and hurt by this. Trying to understand why it had happened she concluded: "I wasn't good enough."

From then on she thought that by becoming good enough, others would regard her with kindness and warmth. So she was polite and agreeable, avoiding confrontations and fulfilling others' needs. "A good employee" was what supervisors called her, scheduling her for the worst shifts. "A dependable co-worker" was what colleagues called her, dumping their projects on her desk. "A generous neighbor" was what neighbors called her, borrowing her recipes without inviting her to their dinner parties.

This continued for some time. And while others' approval seemed imminent, friendship was superficial and romance fleeting, leaving Dolores frustrated. Trying to understand she concluded: "I'm not good enough."

So she became ever more polite and agreeable, ever more avoidant of confrontation, ever more adept at fulfilling others' needs. "A model employee!" praised supervisors, assigning her extra projects with impossible deadlines. "A great co-worker!" praised colleagues, scapegoating her for their mistakes. "A perfect neighbor!" praised neighbors, borrowing her sauce pans without bothering to return them.

Years passed. And while others' approval seemed assured, friendship had become a sham and romance an illusion. This left Dolores brittle with rage. Trying to understand she concluded: "I'll never be good enough."

Finally one evening after another lonely dinner, she sat rigidly in her car and left it running inside the garage until she was dead.

Point: Placing our worth in others' hands leaves us empty.

16

"PERFECTIONISM"

Definition: *Fixing impossible, unreasonable, or grandiose standards of achievement as the price of worth.*

Common Manifestations:
- Childhood wherein rigid, achievement-based expectations are conditional for love and acceptance. The child learns that he/she is not worthy of love unless such expectations are met.

- Excessive goal fixation.

- Obsessing about picayune details.

- A means of belittling, punishing, or controlling others by withholding approval or criticizing 'failure.'

- Value system in which "perfection" is at the pinnacle despite creating only dissatisfaction.

- Lack of empathy.

Sample Distorted Thoughts/Beliefs:
- *"Mommy/daddy will only love me if I'm the best."*
- *"It's not good/right if it's not perfect."*
- *"Imperfection is unacceptable."*
- *"If it's not perfect, then what's the point?!"*
- *"You have to be perfect to deserve love."*
- *"You are worthless if you're not perfect."*
- *"I/you must be perfect."*

Typical Resulting Emotions:
- Anxiety
- Frustration
- Depression
- Shame
- Arrogance
- Stubbornness
- Hopelessness
- Contempt
- Self-Recrimination
- Depression
- Grandiosity

Example: *"You are worthless if you're not perfect"* creates CONTEMPT which leads to dismissing one's child as a failure.

§

"The Queen's Quest"
An Illustration

A WISE QUEEN WANTED to know the meaning of perfection. She spent her years studying books, scrolls, and treatises the world over. Yet despite the many explications, all seemed slavish or indulgent to her and she felt dissatisfied.

After a lifetime of futile searching the queen was despondent. In desperation she issued a royal proclamation: "Let all who know the meaning of perfection present their claim and receive a reward!" Within days the court was overrun with women and men, old and young, poor and wealthy, unknown and renowned from across the land.

First to present themselves was a pupil: "I have earned the highest grades in the kingdom," she said, waving her transcripts. "Is that not perfection?!" But the queen merely shrugged.

Second came an athlete: "I have achieved victory in every contest," he said, posing his physique. "Is that not perfection?!" But the queen merely sighed.

After him was a housewife: "I have the tidiest home in the kingdom," she said, twirling her broom. "Is that not perfection?!" But the queen merely frowned.

A mathematician followed: "I have solved every known equation," he said, hefting reams of calculations. "Is that not perfection?!" But the queen merely shook her head.

Next was an artist: "I have mastered every painting style," she said, unveiling a grand collage. "Is that not perfection?!" But the queen merely dabbed her brow.

Finally came a pastor: "I have saved my whole flock from hellfire," he said, raising his arms toward the heavens. "Is that not perfection?!" But the queen merely rolled her eyes.

Then she saw the line of subjects stretched across the courtyard, out the castle gates, and around the distant bend and dreaded what lay in store. "No, no, no!" she cried. "I've read all this before in books and scrolls and treatises the world over! Does <u>no one</u> know the meaning of perfection?!"

In despair she was about to dismiss them when a young woman shuffled forward. Her blonde hair hung from her skull like old rope, framing wide blue eyes and cadaverous face. Her ribs and hip bones seemed to strain against her threadbare dress. The queen looked at her impatiently.

"Your highness," the young woman began, "I once thought I knew what perfection was. Each day I ate a single piece of bread and drank a single cup of water in perfect measure, and watched myself become perfectly thin." Tears crept down her cheeks. Then she lifted the sticks of her arms overhead, and extended her bony leg in a pose. "Is <u>that</u> not perfection?" she said in a tone that mocked herself.

Exhausted by this effort, the young woman sank to the flagstones. "I'm sorry to have wasted your time," she said. But the queen's gaze had softened, and she held the woman gently in her arms. For at last she knew the meaning of perfection.

Point: Vain opinions full of boasting or begging have much to be desired.

17

"PERSONALIZING"

Definition: *1) Perception that one must be the reason for misfortune or others' behavior; OR 2) Belief that others' dislike diminishes one's worth.*

Common Manifestations:
- Indicates an egocentric ("I am central") mindset that is blind to perspectives other than one's own, or causations besides oneself.

- Poor self-esteem

- Defense against feelings of inadequacy through a convoluted sense of personal significance ("I must matter if I'm the cause or object of...").

Sample Distorted Thoughts/Beliefs:

- *"My wife/husband is angry because of me."*
- *"Service is slow because the waiter doesn't like me."*
- *"She didn't return my phone call right away because she didn't want to talk to me."*
- *"I didn't get the job because the interviewer was out to get me!"*
- *"My son wouldn't have died if I'd been a better father."*
- *"Life is against me!"*
- *"Something must be wrong with me if he/she doesn't like me."*

Typical Resulting Emotions:

- Anger
- Anxiety
- Suspicion
- Depression
- Frustration
- Guilt
- Shame
- Pessimism
- Grandiosity
- Resentment
- Bitterness
- Paranoia

Example: *"Service is slow because the waiter doesn't like me!"* creates RESENTMENT which leads to leaving a nastygram on the check instead of a tip.

°

Note: A common worry here is the "what if" scenario: *"What if the interviewer was out to get me?" or "What if those people are laughing at me?" or "What if that driver meant to cut me off?"*

Rationally these speculations must allow for equally possible alternatives: *"The interviewer <u>wasn't</u> out to get me" or "Those people <u>aren't</u> laughing at me" or "That driver <u>didn't</u> mean to cut me off."* Facing uncertainty about what is true, curiosity or indifference would be logical.

But logic isn't our forte in these situations. In fact our minds readily imagine hurtful possibilities for understandable reasons. Suppressing our anxiety about them tends not to work well or for long. We can, however, tease apart the perceived threat by asking ourselves, "Why is it significant?" or "What does it matter?"

These sorts of encounters chafe mostly because we resent even the possibility that others might not like us. This is of course understandable: who doesn't want to be liked? But perhaps we can discern how legitimate someone's *opinion* of us really is. Must we accept it as the final arbiter of our worth?

Inevitably we won't always be everyone's favorite teddy bear. Then we might ask ourselves, "What does it matter?" Perhaps the answer can be, "It doesn't."

"Shame and the Boy"
An Illustration

AS A CHILD, JACOB heard that he always was to blame for others' mistreatment of him. When his parents abused him, they said it was because he was rotten. When his schoolmates bullied him, they said it was because he was ugly. When his teachers humiliated him, they said it was because he was stupid. Not understanding the true reasons for these things, Jacob felt ashamed.

By the time he reached adulthood, Jacob was used to others' blame for how they mistreated him. Whenever his boss abused him, he said it was because Jacob was lazy. Whenever his neighbors bullied him, they said it was because he was a wuss. Whenever his wife humiliated him, she said it was because he was pathetic. Not understanding the true reasons for these things, Jacob's shame worsened.

Eventually Jacob assumed others' blame even when things had nothing to do with him. Each time his boss grew angry, Jacob <u>knew</u> it was toward him. Each time his neighbors laughed together, he <u>knew</u> it was at him. Each time his wife was unhappy, he <u>knew</u> it was because of him. Not understanding the true reasons for these things, Jacob's shame burned.

So when his boss fired him, Jacob blamed himself. When his neighbors ostracized him, he blamed himself. When his wife divorced him, he blamed himself.

Then without ado, he walked to the nearest busy intersection, looked both ways, and stepped into oncoming traffic.

Point: We needn't crucify ourselves on the cross of others' vileness.

18

"POLARIZING"

Definition: *Viewing things as all-or-nothing and black-and-white instead of some-or-something and shades of grey.*

Common Manifestations:

- Denigration of others as wholly bad if they are not, in one's opinion, wholly good.

- Self-sabotage via limiting options or false choices.

- Indicated by absolute, unrealistic qualifiers such as *always* and *never.*

Sample Distorted Thoughts/Beliefs:

- *"People either love you or hate you."*
- *"It's my way or the highway."*
- *"There's only one way to make a relationship work."*
- *"He <u>always</u> makes a mess of things!"*
- *"She <u>never</u> does anything right!"*
- *"You're either for me or against me."*
- *"If I can't get an 'A' in the class, then it's not worth trying."*

Typical Resulting Emotions:

- Anger
- Frustration
- Vindictiveness
- Anxiety
- Arrogance
- Suspicion
- Self-Righteousness
- Stubbornness
- Bitterness

Example: *"He always makes a mess of things!"* creates FRUSTRATION which leads to yelling at one's husband for leaving a dirty dish in the sink.

§

"The Prince and His Subjects"
An Illustration

IN AN ANCIENT LAND dwelled a young prince whose parents bickered wildly. "If you don't do things my way," they would scream at each other, "then you don't love me!" Whenever the prince misbehaved, they would scream at him too.

Soon the prince began to act the way his parents did. "If you don't do things my way," he would scream at his playmates, "then you don't love me!" This occurred often, and with each tantrum his social circle shrank until he was alone. "It's okay," he told himself, "they didn't love me anyway." Still, he felt sad.

Years passed and the prince married. "If you don't do things my way," he warned his new bride, "then you don't love me!" The princess thought this was absurd and tried to reason with him. But the prince became angry, threatening to imprison her in his dungeon. So one night after he fell asleep, she fled never to return. Upon awakening, the prince realized he was alone again. "It's okay," he told himself, "she didn't love me anyway." Still, he felt sad.

Eventually the prince inherited the kingdom. Yet he soon discovered that his parents had squandered its wealth. Little gold was left to pay his soldiers, or silver to buy goods, or copper for improvements. So he imposed levies. But his impoverished subjects could not pay and protested in the streets.

This enraged the prince. "If you don't do things my way," he screamed at them, "then you don't love me!" First he arrested the leaders to make them obey. Then he imprisoned anyone he could find. This caused the rest to pile their belongings onto wagons, and throw bundles over shoulders as they fled.

Finally the prince had no subjects left and was alone once more. "It's okay," he told himself, "they didn't love me anyway." Still, he felt sad.

Point: Life's realities lay between our extremes.

19

"SHOULDS & SHOULDN'TS"

Definition: *Rules, expectations, or requirements based on dubious opinions, preferences, or traditions.*

Common Manifestations:
- Conformity to perceived authorities regardless of legitimate needs, viable options, necessary changes, or beneficial alternatives.

- A means of pernicious influence.

- Avoidance of guilt or anxiety by clinging to petty moral notions.

Sample Distorted Thoughts/Beliefs:
- *"You shouldn't question authority."*

- *"I shouldn't disobey my husband."*
- *"Good little boys/girls shouldn't think bad thoughts."*
- *"You shouldn't defy conventional wisdom."*
- *"I should just accept things as they are."*
- *"I shouldn't go against what my parents want for me."*
- *"You should do what I want."*
- *"A good person shouldn't become angry."*

Typical Resulting Emotions:
- Fear
- Arrogance
- Guilt
- Anxiety
- Complacency
- Depression
- Timidity
- Smugness
- Resentment
- Anger
- Self-Righteousness

Example: *"A good person shouldn't become angry"* creates GUILT which leads to compulsively attending church instead of enjoying a weekend of fishing.

"The Feuding Busybodies"
An Illustration

TWO CLANS, called Shoulds and Shouldn'ts, moved into a peaceful suburb. Before long the neighbors noticed how alike they were despite their supposed differences. Both drove sensible cars, fastidiously trimmed their lawns, and liked to tell each other how things should or shouldn't be done.

Each morning when Mr. Should walked outside to fetch the newspaper, he saw Mr. Shouldn't across the street trimming his flowers. "You should water them first!" Mr. Should would say cheerfully. And Mr. Shouldn't would reply, "No I shouldn't!"

Each noonday when Mrs. Shouldn't went to the grocery store, she saw Mrs. Should shopping down the aisle. "You shouldn't buy that brand!" Mrs. Shouldn't would say cheerfully. And Mrs. Should would reply, "Oh, yes I should!"

Each evening when Mr. Shouldn't reclined on his front porch, he saw Mr. Should across the street trimming his flowers. "You shouldn't trim them at night!" he would say cheerfully. And Mr. Should would reply, "Oh, yes I should!"

This went on for months until the clans resented each other. "Those Shoulds shouldn't be telling us what to do!" barked Mr. Shouldn't at his wife one evening. And she replied, "Shouldn't we just ignore them, dear?" Meanwhile, across the street Mr. Should barked at _his_ wife, "Those Shouldn'ts should just mind their own business!" And Mrs. Should replied, "Should we just ignore them, dear?"

But the next morning when Mr. Should walked outside to fetch the paper, he saw Mr. Shouldn't across the street trimming his flowers. "You should water them first!" he said cheerfully. And Mr. Shouldn't replied, "No I shouldn't!" Then he stomped over to where Mr. Should was standing with his paper, and yanked it out of his hands. "You shouldn't tell me what to do!" he said. And Mr. Should replied, "Oh, yes I should!"

Then the two lunged at each other, grappling and struggling on the lawn that was trimmed so fastidiously. And the neighbors marveled at how alike they were despite their supposed differences.

Point: Mindless exhortations prescribe what we'd rather avoid, and proscribe what we'd rather enjoy.

20

"VICTIM STANCE"

Definition: *1) Blaming others for the consequences of one's own choices; OR 2) holding others responsible for the nature of one's own thoughts, feelings, and behaviors; OR 3) regarding oneself as ever a victim after having been victimized.*

Common Manifestations:

- "Poor me" mindset wherein one thinks everyone else is better off.

- A means of avoiding guilt/shame by holding others accountable for one's own abusive behaviors.

- A "helplessness" mindset wherein misfortunes are seen as proof of one's powerlessness.

- "No Win" belief that others can solve problems caused by one's choices; yet because one's choices are causing the problems, they can only be solved by oneself.

Sample Distorted Thoughts/Beliefs:
- *"He/she/they/it made me do it."*
- *"She pushed my buttons!"*
- *"My parents screwed me up for good."*
- *"The system is keeping me down."*
- *"Poor me."*
- *"It doesn't matter what I do, so fuck it!"*
- *"I'm stuck in a dead-end job!"*
- *"He/she put bad thoughts into my head!"*

Typical Resulting Emotions:
- Self-Pity
- Anger
- Anxiety
- Vindictiveness
- Frustration
- Bitterness
- Self-Righteousness
- Apathy
- Depression
- Resentment
- Pessimism
- Hopelessness
- Paranoia

Example: *"I'm stuck in a dead-end job!"* creates APATHY which leads to drinking oneself into a stupor night after night in front of the TV.

§

"The Malcontent and His Wife"
An Illustration

RECENTLY MARRIED, Rodney was already frustrated. His wife refused to fold his t-shirts into the tidy squares he liked. And the more he insisted the more she resisted. One morning he'd had enough. "You lazy cow!" he screamed, hurling a t-shirt at her. Then remorse set in and he whined, "See what you made me do?"

Soon Rodney's wife refused to load the dishwasher the way he liked. And the more he insisted the more she resisted. One morning he'd had enough. "You lazy cow!" he screamed, hurling a bowl at her. Then remorse set in and he whined, "See what you made me do?"

Time passed, and Rodney's wife refused to iron the drapes as he liked. And the more he insisted the more she resisted. One morning he'd had enough. "You lazy cow!" he screamed, hurling the iron at her. Then remorse set in and he whined, "See what you made me do?"

Eventually Rodney's wife refused to poach his eggs as he liked. And the more he insisted the more she resisted. One morning he'd had enough. "You lazy cow!" he screamed, about to hurl his hardboiled egg at her.

Suddenly Rodney's wife snatched up a fork and stuck it in his arm. Then remorse set in and she whined, "See what you made me do?"

Point: Wretchedness is crying about the blowback from our abusiveness.

21

"WISHFUL THINKING"

Definition: *Regarding things as one wants them to be rather than as they are.*

Common Manifestations:

- Viewing fantasy as glamorous, and reality as boring.

- Self-sabotage wherein one compulsively makes foolish, wish-based choices *because* of the problems they create.

- Stubborn adherence to an ideology, custom, or tradition that one regards as superior despite its failure to adequately address one's needs or circumstances.

Sample Distorted Thoughts/Beliefs:

- *"People can be counted on to do the right thing."*
- *"My husband will stop hitting me if I'm good."*
- *"Love conquers all!"*
- *"No need to save for retirement—I'll be taken care of somehow."*
- *"Time heals all wounds."*
- *"Once we're married, everything will be wonderful!"*
- *"The more I spend, the more I save."*

Typical Resulting Emotions:

- Euphoria
- Stubbornness
- Complacency
- Frustration
- Recklessness
- Anxiety
- Desperation

Example: *"Once we're married, everything will be wonderful!"* creates EUPHORIA which leads to ignoring a fiancée's cheating.

"The Buyers and Their Debt"
An Illustration

ON BLACK FRIDAY, the orgy of Indebtedness was begun. "Buy, buy, and all will be well!" the high priests intoned.

So people blew their paychecks on overpriced movie tickets, expensive dinners, and trendy gadgets. Then they used credit cards to buy fashionable jewelry, designer clothes, and vacation packages. Finally they mortgaged homes to buy houseboats, sexy cars, and timeshares. In truth they bought what they could with a biblical zeal. And at festival's end the high priests blessed them, and the people slept a righteous sleep.

Each fall, the people indulged this ritual and anticipated the well-being it promised. Yet as time passed they noticed their leisure hours shortening, their work hours lengthening to pay for what they'd bought.

"Is this the promised well-being?" people wondered. But the high priests intoned, "Buy,

buy, and all will be well!" So the people bought with a renewed faith.

Over decades, however, the people watched in dismay as their enjoyment grew scant, their labor arduous, their lives wracked by stress. Bills were stacked like skyscrapers. Some dared wonder if the call to buy had become a siren song.

"Is this the promised well-being?" they asked in dismay. And once more the high priests intoned, "Buy, buy and all will be well!" So the people bought despite their misgivings.

Then came the Buypocalypse! For so long people had borrowed so much that the bills finally crushed them. Businesses fired workers by the millions while millions more lost their homes. Towns and countries went bankrupt. And the high priests repossessed the people's things with a biblical zeal.

"Is this the promised well-being?!" people cried. But the high priests intoned, "Buy, buy and all will be well!" So the people bought what they could until they begged in the streets. And the high priests blessed them, and the people slept a righteous sleep.

Point: False accounting and foolish hope are the severest form of child's play.

PART 2

DISTORTED THINKING
TRANSFORMATION

It is not the mountain we conquer, but ourselves.

Sir Edmund Hillary
(1919 – 2008 C.E.)

1

Self-Awareness

IS IT POSSIBLE TO CHANGE our minds? Consider how often we've done that about trivial things like which outfit to wear, what entrée to order, that perfect dessert, and so on. Yet we do this with important matters too: Switching careers to pursue what we enjoy; going back to school after swearing we'd never do homework again; or deciding that smoking is no longer cool in order to quit.

Sometimes we are influenced by the perspective and insight of others. Or we may weigh the costs and benefits ourselves. Often our emotions push us in one direction or another for reasons we're unaware of. Whatever the case, we clearly can change our minds (which is another way of saying that we can change our thoughts) about many things. In fact, we do it so easily much of the time that we take this ability for granted.

While transforming our distorted thinking isn't quite so effortless, it can be done because it's still just thinking. But an axiom applies: *We must acknowledge the issue before it can be addressed.* This makes sense; yet many of us assume we can enjoy a greater quality of life without quality control. So cultivating self-awareness is crucial.

Not that we don't have bits of it already. If a friend asks us "what's wrong?" for instance, we might reply with "nothing" despite feeling the horns of a dilemma because we don't want to talk about it. Or if our company freezes pay, we can probably finger our resentment while remaining mute to keep our job. And when pulled over for speeding, we usually know how far over the limit we'd hoped to get away with. Yet awareness of our distorted thinking eludes us. Consequently we suffer the distressing emotions and dysfunctional behaviors such thinking creates.

Take Carl and Julia: he's an overworked data analyst, she an underpaid school teacher. Well past their relationship's honeymoon phase, they schedule a "Date Night" dinner each Friday to fan the flame of their romance. On this occasion Carl was harangued by his boss right before his shift ended, and is feeling dour in time to meet Julia at the restaurant.

She instantly reacts to his "attitude" with irritation and wariness. He in turn feels resentment and hurt at her "mood swing." Neither are aware of their emotions beyond a vague discontent, but if pressed would blame each other for "making" them feel this way.

Here's a recap of their dinner talk:

CARL: What did I do now?!
JULIA: What are you talking about?!
CARL: Well, you're obviously upset.
JULIA: *(Upset now)* I'm not upset. You're the one who's mad.
CARL: *(Mad now)* I'm not mad!
JULIA: Obviously you are.
CARL: I am not!
JULIA: Whatever. I'm not upset!
CARL: *(Sighs)* Can we please just order?
JULIA: Fine.

The two pass their meal in strained silence, skip dessert, and go home. Carl buries his head in the TV while Julia updates her online dating profile (not really, but she's pretty frustrated), grades some papers, and goes to bed alone. (If you weren't keeping score that's Dysfunction 1, Romance 0.)

Things didn't need to happen this way! Had these two been self-aware enough to track their emotional reactions and the distorted thinking causing them, they could have transformed their "realities" of each other instead of thrashing about. This would have led to dinner *with* dessert and who-knows-what-else upon arriving home.

While such an alternate "happy ending" might seem simplistic given the complexity of our relationships, it is entirely possible. And it starts with the systematic development of self-awareness. Yet a caveat exists. Despite our potential to become highly self-aware with practice, realizing it is a challenge. Not only do we resist its cultivation (out of chronic repression of thoughts and feelings, or aversion to acknowledging anything undesirable about ourselves, or simple psychological inertia); but we also tend to be so focused on external realities that we neglect our internal workings. These distractions often include entertainment and (bad) news media, consumption of material goods, career and financial concerns, interpersonal relationships, and recreational pursuits.

We are often so enamored of these that we'll look to them exclusively for our quality of life. Granted, our moods *are* enlivened by a witty sit-com or compelling film; we *do* experience peace of mind from having a good job and financial security; our lives *are* enriched by significant others, vacations to unique places, or enjoyable pastimes. And who hasn't experienced the real if short-lived thrill of buying a bigger flat-screen TV or the latest designer handbag and heels?

Unfortunately those preoccupations can't help us if distorted thinking is causing problems in our lives. The only effective recourse, in fact, is cultivating awareness of the self.

2

Practicing Self-Awareness

W E DO THIS BY systematically attending to the five observable aspects of ourselves: breathing, body, senses, emotions, and thoughts. Thus we train the part of our mind that makes us self-aware.

Equate this mental function to a muscle: it needs regular exercise to grow. And like the body, for which an overall warm-up enhances isolated movements, our awareness of distorted thinking is increased by the progressive observation of those other elements first.

Step 1: Focus On Your Breathing

Make yourself comfortable and close your eyes. Inhale deeply through your nose; exhale fully through your mouth. Take a second deep breath, followed by a third. Now breathe normally for several moments, focusing on the rhythm of your breathing. Notice the muscles involved—diaphragm, chest, and neck. Do they feel tense or constricted? If so, try to relax them so your breathing feels less forced.

Next, determine whether your chest or your stomach moves primarily as you breathe. (You may find it helpful to place one hand on each of these areas to discern this.) If your breathing is chest-centered, try to bring your inhaled breath far down into your diaphragm. This is called "deep" breathing, and will cause your stomach to expand and contract more than your chest. Notice how breathing this way feels. Also experiment with "shallow" breathing by keeping the breath high in your chest. You might notice that "deep" breathing feels more relaxing, while "shallow" breathing feels more stimulating or stressful.

After focusing on your breathing for a couple of minutes, shift awareness to your body.

Step 2: "Check In" With Your Body

Are your muscles tense or sore? Do your bones or joints ache? Does any part of your body feel uncomfortable? Depending on whether you are standing, sitting, or lying down, feel the different parts of your body in contact with the surfaces around you.

Now flex and relax each muscle group in turn, starting with your feet. Squeeze, hold for a count of three, and relax. Take a deep breath. Repeat for your calves, thighs, butt, stomach, chest, shoulders, arms, and neck sequentially. Notice how you begin to feel during this exercise.

After observing your body for a couple of minutes, shift awareness to your senses.

Step 3: Experience Your Five Senses

Beginning with your sense of hearing, notice the different sounds in your vicinity. Some will be obvious depending on where you are (traffic, air-conditioning, people talking); others may take care to notice if you tend to ignore them in your day-to-day activities (the soft hum of fluorescent lights), or if they are subtle (your own breathing or heartbeat).

Next, smell the air for different scents around you. This may take more than a few seconds if you don't normally assess your environment this way (except in restaurants, bathrooms, or dental offices).

Third is your sense of sight. Open your eyes and observe everything around you including shapes, colors, textures, patterns, designs, dimensions, and configurations. Notice larger objects first (walls, trees, paintings, people) followed by minute details we often miss (drywall bumps, paint textures, the veins of leaves, the thickness of shoe soles). Close your eyes and notice what you can see behind your eyelids (darkness, shades of red and orange, spots and patterns). Keep your eyes closed for the remainder of the exercise.

Fourth is your sense of taste. Notice any lingering flavors in your mouth (garlic from your last meal, stale cigarettes). Then run your tongue over your teeth, gums, and the fleshy soft palate to experience their shapes and textures.

Finally connect to your sense of touch. Note the texture of your fingertips; the fabric of your clothing and your body's warmth beneath it; the smoothness of a leather armrest or the roughness of fabric. Clasp your hands together as if greeting an old friend. Appreciate your hands' sensitivity and strength, having touched so much in your lifetime.

After experiencing your senses, shift awareness to your emotions.

Step 4: Feel Your Emotions

To better connect with these you might ask yourself, "How am I feeling right now?" Simply observe whatever emotions are present without doing anything with them.

Imagine that your emotions are like children playing in the park, and you are the watchful but indulgent parent. Rather than telling them how to play or forbidding it, simply allow them to *be*. This may feel challenging if you tend to act heedlessly on your emotions, or suppress them for whatever reason, or judge yourself for feeling certain ones such as anger.

Cultivating an attitude of *nonjudgment* toward our emotions, while difficult, is vital. They are a natural element of our psycho-emotional functioning as well as an essential medium through which we experience life. So acknowledging them is both sensible and beneficial. Not only do we validate an important part of us (which is crucial to psychological well-being), but we create an opportunity to identify the cognitive source of those emotions.

People commonly wonder, "Shouldn't I suppress emotions such as anger or resentment? Aren't they destructive?" Understanding the difference between *emotions* and *actions* is important. Emotions alone cannot harm others or cause destruction in the world (though of course they can trouble one's own mind). Put another way, it's not how we feel but what we *do* with those feelings that matters—and we aren't required to do anything with a feeling. In that sense no emotion is "bad," even ones that disturb us (such as fear); nor are we "bad" for feeling them, even those commonly condemned (such as anger). And because distressing emotions are usually *symptoms* of distorted thinking, dismissing them actually prevents our addressing that underlying cause and thus healing the emotional state.

After spending a few minutes on your emotions, shift awareness to your thoughts.

Step 5: Observe Your Thoughts

As with your emotions, you might find it helpful to ask yourself, "What am I thinking right now?" Try to observe these, too, with an attitude of *nonjudgment.*

Imagine that your thoughts are like a river. At times it may drift or babble or surge, reflecting the seasonal mood. Rather than trying to divert the river's flow or dam it altogether, allow it to churn past as you sit quietly on its banks in the knowledge that you have chosen not to be swept away by it.

Recognize that your thoughts—beliefs, attitudes, perspectives, and the significance you assign to things, all arising in response to countless experiences over a lifetime—are a unique and inevitable product of your mind. This is true whether or not you agree with or want them. So they are a natural, valid part of you in this moment. You can either deny or condemn them out of fear and self-rejection, or accept and observe them toward developing insight into their nature.

Also, note the crucial difference between *thoughts* and *behavior.* By themselves thoughts cannot harm others or cause destruction in the world—though ones we find troubling or disturbing can certainly cause us distress. Yet that likely wouldn't be the case if not for the misguided belief that such thoughts are "bad," or that one is "bad" for thinking them, or that their mere presence is somehow of dire significance. Who has not, from time to time, projected scenes of violence, mayhem, or desolation in the private theater of their imagination? Yet these showings, like the movies, remain mere fantasy.

You've probably noticed that thoughts often arise irrespective of whether they are rational or conducive to a sense of well-being. Do you sometimes lie awake at night for hours because your mind churns them out like beaters in a mixing bowl? Such mental activity isn't helpful but that doesn't prevent it.

Realize that the mind's tendency to generate thoughts prolifically is normal. Investigating, analyzing, synthesizing, remembering, and finally understanding ourselves, others, circumstances, and the world are difficult and sometimes overwhelming tasks. So simply observe your thoughts—no matter their aspect or number—as they flow unimpeded through your mind while you remain still and calm. How does it feel to disregard the "need" to *do something right now* with your thoughts? Do you realize that your thoughts are "just thoughts"—mercurial, paradoxical, compulsive, or irrational *products* of the mind—rather than infallible and immutable reflections of yourself?

After observing your thoughts for a few minutes, return attention to your breathing. Inhale and exhale deeply once again. Do you feel different from when you started? Now open your eyes. This concludes the self-awareness exercise.

3

Applying Self-Awareness

A S SELF-AWARENESS INCREASES, you'll notice "flashes" of distorted thoughts in your mind. Also, certain of your emotions and behaviors may puzzle you because of their over-reactive or otherwise dubious characteristics. Curiosity about this is natural. And questions such as "Why am I feeling so strongly about *that*?" or "Why would I do such a thing?!" are essential because those kinds of responses tend to indicate distorted thinking.

Given how readily the mind conceals such, it is easier at times to notice these emotional and behavioral symptoms first before backtracking to their cognitive root. This is typically the case with deep-seated beliefs. In this we are like mental detectives—

investigators of our own minds—who sift the emotional and behavioral clues we ourselves leave behind.

To see how this process works, let's accompany Carl and Julia on another date night. Carl is feeling dour again after his boss's harangue. Julia, noticing his mood, immediately reacts with irritation and wariness. But because she's been practicing her self-awareness exercise, she notices her emotional response to Carl *as it occurs* (although she hasn't yet placed the distorted thinking underlying it). Now she has the presence-of-mind to realize that her emotional reaction is a bit much for the circumstances.

At this point she backtracks from her emotional reaction by asking herself, *"Why am I feeling this way?"* She wants to identify the thinking that is causing her emotional response. Sure enough, a thought flashes into her awareness: *"He's mad at me."* Suddenly Julia understands her emotional reaction; it even makes sense given the "reality" her mind has presented. Simultaneously she recognizes that her thinking is distorted because she's making Carl's mood about her without evidence to support that conclusion (Personalizing).

Meanwhile, Carl has just seen Julia's mood shift; he feels his resentment and hurt wash over him. But because he, too, has been practicing his self-awareness exercise he is able to note the exaggerated nature of these emotions. Then he asks himself, *"Why am I feeling this way?"* The thought that flashes for him is *"She's bored with me."* Suddenly he understands his emotional reaction, and recognizes that he is both "Personalizing" and "Jumping to Conclusions" in the form of mind-reading.

For Carl, increased self-awareness gives him the wherewithal to ask his wife about her mood (a novel idea). As this would give Julia a chance to share the true reason for her feelings, Carl's "reality" would change for the better, as would hers. (And they might share a laugh at the absurdity of it all.)

Note that Carl and Julia wisely avoid the three mistakes that people commonly make in this process: 1) Never questioning their emotional reactions, even when they (and the actions likely to follow) spell "T-R-O-U-B-L-E"; 2) Immediately suppressing or rejecting those emotional reactions if a part of their mind views them as irrational, undesirable, or problematic; and 3) Blaming the other person for "making" them feel this way.

Remember that our emotions in a given situation are products of, and thus clues to, *our own* thinking. So the only way we can backtrack from an emotional state to find the underlying distorted thinking is to first notice the emotion itself. This psychological maneuver requires *acceptance*, not rejection, of our emotion in that moment. Such acceptance in turn allows an open-minded inquiry into that emotion's source.

Summary of this process:
1. *Observe your emotion ("How am I feeling?").*
2. *Investigate your emotion's cognitive root ("Why am I feeling this way?").*
3. *Identify your distorted thought.*

°

*Note: Exploring the deep, dark psychological roots of one's distorted thinking is not strictly necessary to transform it; rather, recognition that the thinking is distorted can alone be enough. Julia's tendency to personalize Carl's dourness, for example, could have several possible origins. It might have begun in childhood when she made her father's dourness about herself through egocentricity. Or it might have started during a prior relationship with a dourly abusive boyfriend. Perhaps it began at some other time in her life where dourness was a burden. (Speculation of this sort could be made about Carl's distorted thinking as well.) Ultimately when, where, why, or how the distorted thinking started is beside the point: now it is changeable.

However, such exploration sometimes provides a motivating rationale *("I learned to think this way because of childhood abuse, not because it was ordained at birth")* for starting the difficult work of change. Insight then becomes essential.

4

Distorted Thought Challenge

Wouldn't IT BE NICE if we could catch and correct our distorted thinking once and be done with it? But creating lasting change, as you might expect, is more involved because such thinking is habitual and entrenched.

So a structured psychoeducational process similar to formal schooling is required. But instead of academic subjects, we are learning new ways of thinking. And rather than being taught in a classroom, we are teaching ourselves in the forum of our own lives.

°

Step 1: Write the Distorted Thought.

By fixing the distorted thought on paper, we make tangible something that otherwise can be difficult to identify or recall because of its mercurial and self-camouflaging aspects. Have you ever forgotten brilliant ideas or insightful dreams because you failed to write them down? Imagine if Da Vinci, Einstein, or Edison hadn't recorded the revolutionary notions about art, science, or invention that often came to them like lightning.

- **Example:** "I am a failure."

Step 2: Identify the Distorted Thinking Pattern(s).

This is vital for two reasons: 1) It encourages familiarization with these patterns, which makes them easier to identify; and 2) It confirms that the thought is, in fact, distorted because the criteria have been met. Such reinforcement is helpful, particularly at the start of this process, because our distorted thinking feels familiar, natural, and "right" even as our rational mind begins to recognize it for what it is. Write this below the distorted thought.

- **Example:** "I am a failure."
  - **Distorted Thinking Pattern(s):**
    "Disqualifying the Positive"
    "Perfectionism"
    "Polarizing"

Step 3: Find the Distorted Thinking Flaws.

Explore all the reasons why the thought is, in fact, distorted. The *pattern(s)* of distorted thinking you've identified will guide you here. Write this below the types.

- **Example:** "I'm a failure."
  - **Distorted Thinking Pattern(s):**

"Disqualifying the Positive"
"Perfectionism"
"Polarized Thinking"

- **Thinking Flaws:** 1) The thought is too general, fails to consider my successes (great or small); 2) How do I define "failure"? One mistake? Two? More? Is there *anyone* who hasn't made a mistake or "failed" to achieve a goal at some point in their lives? Are *they* failures? Would I call Edison a "failure" because he "failed" so many times before finally creating the light bulb? 3) Am I applying a standard of "failure" to myself that I would not apply to others? If so, is that rational or fair? Why would I do that to myself? 4) Is there a difference between "failing" and being a "failure"? How do I decide the difference? 5) How did I choose the definition of "failure" that I'm applying to myself? Is that the only possible definition? Is it merely an opinion? 6) Why am I emphasizing my "failures" instead of my successes? Does success matter less? Why not emphasize that instead?

Step 4: Choose a Better Thought.

We have the power to exercise more beneficial thinking than what we now claim as ours. But to facilitate this psychological shift, the new thought must have three characteristics: 1) It *directly* negates the distorted thought or belief; 2) It is a notion that one's own rational mind can accept as valid (even if it *feels* wrong); and 3) It is more beneficial and empowering than the distorted thought being replaced.

Once you have chosen your new thought, write it directly opposite the distorted thought on your paper. This juxtaposition forces your mind to confront both thoughts simultaneously (essentially creating cognitive dissonance *purposely* to catalyze change). Because one negates the other, your rational mind will naturally choose the more functional, beneficial, and mentally healthy of the two.

- **Example:**
  - "I am a failure." / "I am a success."

      or
      / "I am successful."
      or
      / "I can 'fail' and still succeed."
      Etc.

Step 5: Support the Better Thought.

Even as your rational mind recognizes the new belief's validity, you will likely need to explore why it is valid in order to *feel* okay about proceeding further. This exploration might include examples of actual accomplishments, sound opinions or rationales that resonate, or additional compelling evidence. Write these after the new thought.

- **Example:** "I am a success."
    1) I have achieved goals in my life, such as _____ and _____. 2) My life includes _____ (a good job, a beautiful family, my health, friends, skills, education, good morals, etc.). 3) It is possible to be a success without having achieved *everything* I ever set goals for. 4) I decide what "success" means in *my* life, and for me it means _____. 5) I have overcome

_____ (abusive childhood, lack of education, physical handicap, competition, prejudice, poverty, other misfortunes, etc.)—is that not success?

Step 6: Study the Better Thought.

As with learning anything new, repetition is necessary. Settled wisdom tells us that doing the new activity at least once each day for a rough *minimum* of thirty days is essential to changing a habit. Longer than that is required to reinforce the new habit through additional repetition over time.

Reviewing everything you have written in Steps 1 through 5, while paying particular attention to the better thought and its supporting arguments, three times each day (morning, noon, and night) is a good start. One might well adopt this auto-suggestive approach for as long as it takes to experience the desired results, like any other skill.

In this a marathoner's mindset rather than a sprinter's is necessary. Transforming one's distorted thinking can be as rigorous—though also as rewarding—as learning a musical instrument or foreign language, developing a sound tennis or golf swing, deepening ability in chess or the martial arts, broadening vocational knowledge, earning a degree, cultivating a garden, building a business, and so on. Yet millions of people willingly undertake such pursuits despite the time and effort involved because they know that achievement is worth it.

At the same time, many of us regard the unique work of psychological growth as just too difficult; so we don't begin or, having begun, sustain that process. While it admittedly *is* challenging, much of the angst lies in our naïve expectation that it should be easy simply because it is worthy, and that if it's not easy then something is wrong. But if replacing bad habits with good were inherently painless by virtue of being beneficial, no one would struggle with quitting smoking, losing weight, improving diet, or the many other excellent personal changes that are possible.

Ultimately no pursuit is more worthwhile. Our thoughts are the primary source of feelings and behaviors throughout our lives, and thus determine our capacity for happiness or success in any endeavor.

5

Realizing the Change

C LIENTS OFTEN ASK, "How long does it take to transform distorted thinking?" This is naturally followed by "What does that process look like?"

As to the first inquiry, I'm sure you'll be pleased to read that it's difficult to say. Each person's mind is unique, from entrenchment of thought patterns to motivation for change to potential for psychological healing. Much depends on how diligently one does the exercises outlined in this book.

In addition, both client feedback and my own experience show that some distorted thoughts are readily changed while others take longer. For example, *"This task is impossible!"* tends to be more easily transformed than *"People can't be trusted."* Perhaps this is because the former is narrowly specific, less pervasive while the latter is broadly generalized, applying to *all* people at *all* times in *all* situations.

Not insignificantly, these all-encompassing beliefs are often formed in childhood. We know that childhood belief systems, comprising as they do an essential part of our sense of what is real or true at a highly impressionable stage of life, are typically the most resistant to change. But these overgeneralizing beliefs also appear in response to deeply impactful experiences regardless of age. These include trauma. Someone who nearly dies in a plane crash, for instance, might conclude: *"Flying is too dangerous."* Such a belief, clearly intended to prevent future harm from plane crashes by creating an aversion to flying, exerts tremendous influence and is not readily changed for obvious reasons.

Moreover, we need not bind ourselves with naïve expectations stemming from the desire to transform quickly, or based on some artificial timeframe. Of course it would be great if every skill we learned, every endeavor we pursued, every change we undertook gratified us instantly. But life teaches us that these things cannot be rushed. Given that reality, we do ourselves a favor by accepting it in order to embrace the process of change for which there is no shortcut. (This way of thinking, not surprisingly, needs practice as well.)

It's like taking a road trip. Although we can find the quickest route, push the limits of speed, even drive all night, we are still left with the journey itself—the uncompromising geographical distance—that cannot be circumvented. Passengers who squirm at this tend to become frustrated while making life miserable for others trapped in the car with them. In contrast, those who find ways to pass the time are able to "relax and enjoy the ride." In many other life situations, we accept with grace if not enthusiasm the inevitable and it goes better for us. Why not do the same here?

As to the question, "What does this process look like?" clients report a typical experience that I have also noted in my transformational work. Initially no change seems to be occurring as the distorted thoughts and distressing emotions reverberate. This is the most frustrating phase of the process, understandably, and when many people give up.

With continued reinforcement, however, one starts to experience flashes of the new thought. Here the mind is incorporating the new thinking even as the distorted thought and its emotions predominate.

Gradually these flashes occur more frequently. At some point the emotional distress feels less urgent or acute. Farther along, the new thought appears more strongly and consistently in the mind, not merely flashing but settling in as it were into a new familiarity. Emotionally one still experiences shades of the old discomfort, mitigated considerably by the new thinking that the mind is learning.

This inverse relationship between increasing new-thought frequency and decreasing emotional distress develops steadily. Eventually the troubling emotions no longer compromise one's behavior and well-being. We may find ourselves wondering about this absence, as though it were a phantom itch that we've already scratched—a typical reaction to the loss of something we once routinely experienced.

Summary of this process:

- *Phase 1:* No change evident; distorted thought & distressing emotions reverberate.
- *Phase 2:* Occasional flashes of the new/better thought; distorted thought & distressing emotions predominate.
- *Phase 3:* Frequent flashes of the new/better thought; distorted thought & distressing emotions less compelling.
- *Phase 4:* New/better thought & resulting emotions predominate; distorted thought & distressing emotions recede.
- *Phase 5:* Outward change evident; new/better thought & resulting emotions reverberate.

°

Let's revisit Carl and Julia one last time to see this process in action. After talking with each other about what's going wrong on their date nights, Julia decides to challenge her distorted thought (*"He's mad at me"*) with *"Carl's mood is about him"* (which is true). Carl, in turn, has chosen to challenge his distorted thought (*"She's bored with me"*) with *"Julia still finds me exciting"* (because she does).

Through auto-suggestive reinforcement of their new thoughts, Carl and Julia experience small changes at first. When Carl is feeling dour, Julia still reacts with irritation and wariness. However, her self-awareness coupled with the flash of the new thought in her mind is enough to make her ask Carl about what's going on with him. Meanwhile as Carl feels his own resentment and hurt, his self-awareness coupled with the flash of the new thought in his mind is enough to make him receptive to Julia's overtures of communication. He is able, in turn, to ask about her experience instead of shutting down.

While this is happening, both are aware that their feelings conflict with the way of resolution—a hallmark of the cognitive relearning process. What helps them proceed despite this challenging internal state is the understanding, reinforced through the self-awareness exercise, that their emotions are merely products of distorted thinking rather than infallible aspects of themselves that they "should" or "must" obey. In addition, *practicing the self-awareness exercise has increased their psychological tolerance of this state.*

As time passes, Carl and Julia notice a lessening of their negative emotional reactions to each other. Simultaneously the new thoughts they are learning flash more readily in their minds. Communication is easier. (This progression has the feel of a descending traverse-staircase as the mind toggles between old and new in its ever-deepening learning process.)

At last the moment comes. Carl is feeling dour from the now-customary harangue (and we wonder when he'll decide to find a better job). Julia expects her familiar irritation and wariness. Instead a new thought resounds in her mind: *"His mood is about him."* She experiences a calmness that pleasantly surprises her. Meanwhile Carl sees her tranquil mood and notices himself thinking, *"She still finds me exciting."* He smiles in delight. She smiles back. Then the two enjoy dinner with lively and affectionate conversation. More wine is followed by dessert and, upon arriving home, who knows what else?

CONCLUSION

Knowledge of what is possible
Is the beginning of happiness.

George Santayana
(1863 – 1952 C.E.)

We are star stuff harvesting star light.
Carl Sagan (1934 - 1996 C.E.)

A N UNDERSTANDING of distorted thinking leads to the observation that we humans suffer devaluation in a variety of ways and as a matter of course. Indeed, our perceived worth often mingles with the dregs of society's estimation.

The tragedy is that one's degradation of another and another's acquiescence in such throughout history have reflected the notion that worth is determined by race, gender, culture, class, profession, religion, sexual orientation, or some other inane and arbitrary value judgment.

Note the designations *master* and *slave, patrician* and *plebeian, noble* and *commoner, lord* and *serf, believer* and *infidel, blessed* and *damned, civilized* and *savage, master race* and *mongrel races, blue bloods* and *lowbrows,* patriarchy's *weaker sex,* and the caste system's *untouchables*—even *Conservative* and *Liberal*, once merely indicative of political leaning, now reek of epithet! A primitive and pernicious bias created these distinctions, while grotesque custom and an apparent hangover from the cave perpetuate them. For good reason does George Orwell's barnyard commandment have bite: "All animals are equal, but some animals are more equal than others."

An accepted principle in our material world, wherein value is assigned for doing business, is that things of the same essential makeup have the same intrinsic worth. Gold, for instance, retains a standard value by weight in the market regardless of its form or function on the street. So if one were to say that an ounce of gold is worth more as a coin than a bar, we'd shake our heads. Granted, the coin might have greater *extrinsic*—opinion—value to a coin collector; but that wouldn't alter the fact that, coin or bar, the gold is gold is gold.

With that preface, is it possible to verify an essential makeup common to *us* such that our worth transcends mere prejudice?

It is possible.

First, we are categorized through DNA and physiology inherent to our species. This includes the pigmentation of skin, eyes, and hair according to nature's palette through environmental adaptations over many thousands of years. These no more signify caliber among humans than paint colors show quality among cars!

Second, we are characterized by unique psychological functioning, intelligence, and emotional breadth. While our personality traits and cognitive abilities may range along a spectrum, we all experience an array of emotions including anger and tranquility, sorrow and happiness, indifference and love, contempt and admiration, hatred and compassion, fear and anticipation, despair and hope, as well as the need for respect, understanding, and acceptance.

Third, we are recognized as remaining human—and perhaps rendered more deeply so—despite having been scarred, deformed, or crippled by our hardships. If a rough diamond with its pitted opaqueness is mistaken for chipped glass, does its nature change through misapprehension?

Last, we are uniquely positioned in our species' history to explore the subatomic world—the "building blocks" of all matter in the Universe. There we see that *everything* is made of the same particular fabric, piling proof upon proof of our essential commonality.

But that recognition is only part of our solution. Clearly we are akin to those worldly treasures—gold and silver, precious stones, money, real estate—that have been valued above human life routinely from ancient times. And we share an essential makeup with the sun and moon, while supernovae from eons past seeded the elements we are made of today.

Why does all this matter?

Long ago we worshipped the heavenly bodies as gods because of their radiant beauty, mystery, and power. Now that we know their essence is ours, you'd think our apotheosis would be imminent. Nevertheless the ceiling on our value is vaulted. Let us not fail to utilize that space! For though we are all equally worthy, what *is* that worth? Consider the sun, moon, and stars as you decide.

Special thanks to Michele Y. McWilliams for her perspective, insight, and commentary during the writing of this book. Thanks also to Erin Bassity and Chuck Nilan for their feedback and enthusiasm.

About the Author

Brian M. Keltner received his Master's degree in Counseling Psychology from the University of Denver. He is a Colorado State Licensed (LPC) and Nationally Certified Counselor (NCC) in private practice.

Over the past ten years, Brian has helped many hundreds of clients resolve mental health concerns including depression, anxiety, childhood abuse, anger management, grief-and-loss, relationship problems, domestic violence, interpersonal boundaries, and life-transitions such as divorce, job loss, relocation, retirement, and terminal illness. In addition, as a former U.S. Marine deployed to Mogadishu, Somalia —a city devastated by civil war, famine, mass starvation, and insurgency—he has worked successfully with veterans struggling with PTSD, depression, anger, grief, and suicidal thinking.

Prior to becoming a mental health practitioner, he studied English literature and creative writing at the University of Colorado at Boulder. After earning his Bachelor's degree he taught school in Los Angeles for several years.

Presently Brian counsels individuals and couples in Denver, Colorado. He can be reached via website: www.psychotherapywithanedge.com.

68225067R00107

Made in the USA
Charleston, SC
06 March 2017